Pray Big for
YOUR LIFE

Pray Big for
YOUR LIFE

The Power of Specific and Biblical Prayers

WILL DAVIS JR.

Guideposts
New York, New York

Library of Congress has cataloged Baker Publishing Group's paperback edition of *Faith Set Free* as follows:

Library of Congress Cataloging-in-Publication Data
Davis, Will, 1962–
    Pray big for yourself: pray for yourself with reckless abandon / Will Davis, Jr.
        p.   cm.
    Includes bibliographical references.
    ISBN 978-0-8007-3247-9 (pbk.)
    1. Prayer—Christianity. I. Title.
BV210.3.D37 2009
248.3'2—dc22

                                                                                                  2006037330

Printed in the United States of America
10 9 8 7 6 5 4 3 2 1

To my mother, Ann B. Davis

Contents

Acknowledgments

Thanks to . . .

- Susie—for being a world-class wife
- Will III, Emily, and Sara—for your patience and grace for all the times I was glued to a computer screen
- Steve Carrell—for not being at homecoming
- Julie Apra, Liz Benigno, Terri Crow, Dana Diven, Ron Duncan, Erika Dunham, Ed Frazier, Tonya Parrott, Lorri Payne, Sandra Roche, Dana Roraback, Mike Schatzman, Gary Sinclair, Steve Tyndall, Lynn Walker, and Julie Washington—for helpful comments and insights into personal praying
- The Kampen 242 group—for being generous
- Julie Apra—for being a spiritual warrior
- Derek and Bonnie Buchert—for not quitting when you could have
- Gary Sinclair—for being a great friend and for modeling good Bible study methods

- The ACF overseers and board—for encouraging and allowing me to write
- The ACF executive team and staff—for being my friends and colaborers
- Andrea and Curt Smith—for tireless love, support, and friendship
- Vicki Crumpton—for continued excellent coaching, support, and friendship
- Suzie Cross Burden—for your passionate belief in the Pray Big concept
- The amazing Revell team—Cheryl Van Andel, Twila Bennett, Deonne Beron, Debbie Deacon, Claudia Marsh, Brooke Nolen, Jessica Miles, Karen Steele—for gorgeous covers, excellent editing, first-class promotions, world-class service, and overall outstanding service and support. You are a joy to work with.

Part 1

Learning to Pray
for Yourself

Welcome to *Pray Big for Your Life*. In the following pages, you will learn how to develop a robust faith through personal prayer. You'll discover how to pray big, hairy, audacious prayers for very specific areas of your life. You will also be reminded of some extremely helpful spiritual disciplines that will boost your own personal prayer habits.

In this first part, let's talk about pinpoint praying and why you need to pray specific prayers for yourself.

1

Tired of Just Hanging Around?

Very early in the morning, while it was still dark, Jesus got up, left the house and went off to a solitary place, where he prayed.

Mark 1:35

It's amazing how quickly your prayer life kicks in when you're suspended eighty feet above a rocky riverbank by a thin rope. Actually, suspended and *stuck*. With all that time to gaze at the rocks below, prayer is bound to happen.

When I was a college student, I fell in love with the sport of rappelling. You know, rappelling—you tie a rope onto something really high, run it through a harness on your waist, and then proceed to walk, run, or skip down the face of a sheer drop-off. I actually kept ropes and a harness in my car just in case I saw a ledge, a building, a cliff, a bridge, or a mountain face that was just begging to be walked down.

The hills near my college campus provided a great spot for serious rappelling. The Brazos River flowed about 120 feet below an overhanging cliff. Several large trees and even part of an old wall provided many secure places to which I could tie my rope. After the first few steps down the face of the cliff, the wall dropped away and formed a huge overhang about thirty feet deep. In order to touch the wall, you actually had to swing in big arcs like a giant pendulum. You could get a good forty- or fifty-foot swing going on that overhang. Let me tell you, hanging a hundred feet over the riverbank and acting like a pendulum is quite a wild ride.

And it was the promise of that wild ride that had lured me and a buddy to the cliff early on a Saturday morning. My friend was a rappelling instructor at a Christian camp in the summer, so I felt pretty safe. So safe, in fact, that I decided to go first. I hooked onto the rope, checked my harness, and leaned out over the ledge. I took a couple of quick hops down the face, and then I started my big swinging motions. Few things can compete with the sensation of swinging in the wind over a beautiful riverbank in the fresh morning air.

That is, until I came to a sudden, jerking stop. A small piece of masking tape that I had wrapped around my rappelling rope to mark its seventy-five-foot point got caught in the small safety line I was using. The result was that the safety line locked into place and froze me in midair. It worked too well. I was totally stuck. My weight on the rope kept the safety line taut.

The good news was that I wasn't going to fall. The bad news was that I wasn't going anywhere. I was hanging about eighty feet above the riverbank, with absolutely no way to free myself.

As I hung there, the harness that was wrapped around my waist and thighs began to cut off my circulation. Within a few minutes, I couldn't feel my legs. I knew I was in real trouble.

So, what do you do when you're dangling nearly eight stories above the rocks below? How do you pass the time? After a while, the view got old, so I started thinking. I thought about my friends, my girlfriend, and my parents. I thought about how mad they would all be at me if I didn't come out of this little escapade in one piece. I thought about how stupid I was to not know that the tape would catch on the safety line. And I thought about God. I even talked to him.

Sometimes you have to get really stuck before you realize how much you need God.

Going Nowhere Fast?

Maybe you can relate to being stuck. I don't mean stuck like I was above the river; I mean stuck spiritually, stuck in your relationship with God. I certainly can relate. I know what it feels like to have the spiritual doldrums. When I'm stuck spiritually, I have little or no momentum in my walk with Christ. I know he loves me and that I'm going to heaven, but that's about it.

Some people live years suspended in the Christian life. The view is nice enough—they can see God's kingdom work, they see others moving and growing in their relationships with Christ, and they even have a hope of heaven. They're suspended somewhere between spiritual infancy and becoming a true disciple of Jesus. They're stuck, and their faith is suffering because of it.

So, what's the cure for this spiritual rut? Prayer. That's right—good, biblical, bended-knee prayer. If you want to jolt your life out of its spiritual rut and really begin to see God's presence and power take hold in your relationships, your job, your ministry, and your own attitudes and actions, then start praying for yourself. Even if you're not good at prayer, even if you feel like you tried prayer and failed miserably, even if you don't know where or how to start, don't fret. Prayer is still your answer. You really can learn how to change your life through personal prayer.

Why Pray for Yourself?

I need prayer, and lots of it. Think about it: there is no other person in my life with a greater capacity to impact the work of God in my life than *me*. The same is true for you. This is a critical point, so let me say it very clearly: the person in your life with the greatest capacity to help or hinder God's work in you is *you*. You need to be praying for yourself—your heart, your attitudes, your habits, your relationships, your resources, your temptations, and your ministry—because no other person can or will impact God's kingdom processes in your life as much as you will. For that reason alone, you need to pray every day for yourself.

I'm still amazed when I meet Christ-followers who don't pray for themselves. Somehow they've gotten the idea that it's self-centered to pray for their own needs. But what they don't realize is that by not praying for themselves, they're choosing to live a life of Christian mediocrity, and they're greatly limiting the degree to which they can experience the abundant life Jesus offered (see John 10:10).

Christians who don't pray for themselves aren't being humble or selfless. Rather, they're choosing to greatly limit their spiritual impact. Christians who don't pray about their own needs and lives are the spiritual equivalent of football players who take the field without any protective pads—or, worse, soldiers who run into battle completely unarmed. They're totally set up to fail.

Bless Me Indeed

Let me offer you three great reasons to become a self-intercessor. There are certainly more reasons than just these, some of which we'll touch on later. But these three make up a good theological foundation for why it is necessary to pray for ourselves.

First, we need to pray for ourselves because Jesus prayed for himself. You have to figure that if Jesus felt the need to pray for himself—and he was the perfect, sinless Son of God—then it's reasonable to conclude that we need to pray for ourselves as well. We can actually take that reasoning one step further: maybe Jesus was able to live such an anointed life because he was a man of prayer. Surely his ability to resist temptation, speak with authority, heal the sick, and always choose wisely was due in part to the unbroken communion he felt with God through his unceasing prayers.

In the next chapter, we'll take a close look at why prayer was so important to Jesus. For our purposes here, let's just acknowledge that Jesus found prayer to be his main means of maintaining unbroken fellowship with his Father. Remember, humanity was a new experience for Jesus. He had existed for all eternity in perfect, spiritual communion with God, and then, *wham!*—he wakes up as a crying baby in a manger. He had to learn to relate to God on an entirely new level.

I think Jesus found prayer to be helpful and comforting because it reminded him of his home. There was something about the sweetness and intimacy of prayer that brought him close to heaven. Meaningful moments with God in prayer are one of the ways we can get closest to a heavenly reality on earth. That's why Jesus liked it and made it such a priority in his life.

So doesn't it seem rather obvious that if God's holy Son, the world's only perfect human, felt the need to pray for himself, then we, who are far less than perfect, need prayer for ourselves as well? Doesn't it make sense that if Jesus's perfect soul still needed the comfort that prayer could bring, then our wounded and weary souls need it even more? And doesn't it make sense that if Jesus built his life on the discipline of personal prayer, then we should too?

Jesus was the world's only expert at being human. More than any other person in history, Jesus showed us what humanity was meant to be—and he did so against the backdrop of prayer. If we learn anything from Jesus's amazing life, it's that we as humans need to pray.

Second, we need to pray for ourselves because the Holy Spirit is trying to make us holy. In Philippians 1:6, Paul wrote that God would continue the work of making us pure and holy until we reached heaven. Jesus prayed that we would be sanctified, or made holy, by his Word (see John 17:17). In short, Jesus is making us holy for our eternal home. He promised to present us as his perfect bride to our heavenly Father, but before he can, he has to complete the process of our purification. Prayer is one of the main things we can do to help that process along.

When you pray, especially for yourself, you soften the soil of your heart and make your will more pliable in God's hands. Prayer paves the way for God's Spirit to move and work without hindrance in the deep recesses of your heart. Your personal prayers grant the Spirit permission to mold and reshape you into the image of Jesus.

Isaiah the prophet predicted that there would be a forerunner to Jesus. He said that a messenger would come who would call the nation of Israel to prepare a way for the coming king and to clear a straight path for him. John the Baptist was that messenger (see Luke 3:1–6). He told expectant Hebrews to get their hearts ready for repentance and the baptism of God's Holy Spirit.

Prayer does that too. It prepares the way for the king and makes you ready for the cleansing changes he wants to bring to your life. It's like rolling out the red carpet for the Holy Spirit to walk right into your heart.

To be prayerless, or at least not praying for yourself, is to keep your heart hard and calloused toward the work of God in you. It creates a spiritual environment in your soul that's not conducive to the sanctifying work of God's Spirit in you. It might mean that God has to use a sledgehammer or a two-by-four, rather than his gentle hand, to soften your heart and begin to bring about the changes he wants to make in you. Using the biblical imagery of the potter and the clay, prayer simply makes it easier for God to mold you without breaking you in the process. To me, that's a great reason to pray.

Finally, we need to pray for ourselves because the life that God calls us to live is impossible without prayer. Go read the Sermon on the Mount, Matthew 5–7. Review Jesus's call for us to live kingdom-focused lives: to love our enemies, turn the other cheek, not worry about provisions, not have lustful thoughts, and never judge others inappropriately. Jesus's command is for us to be perfect as his Father is perfect, but the life he challenges us to live is absolutely impossible for any human. Without the anointing and equipping of God's Spirit, we can never live, love, serve, and give as God expects us to.

The religious elite of Jesus's day had turned rule keeping and religious duty into a finely tuned science. If a God-pleasing life could be reached through human effort, then these guys certainly would have been voted "most likely to succeed" in kingdom things. But Jesus rebuked them for their empty religiosity. He actually said that to live a true kingdom life, our righteousness has to exceed that of the religious elite (see Matt. 5:20). Jesus's point was that kingdom living is about living a *received* life, not an *achieved* one. And the life that he wants for us is one that we receive through prayer.

In John 6:63, Jesus taught that his Spirit alone gives life (kingdom life); the flesh (our best efforts) profits nothing. If you are serious about living the biblical and godly life that God calls you to, then you have to live it by the power of his Spirit. The best way to become a Spirit-drenched person is through regular, focused prayer.

In John 15:8, Jesus challenged his disciples to bear much fruit for his glory. He also told them how to live fruit-bearing lives: by abiding in him (see John 15:4–5). Prayer tethers you to God. It drives the tent pegs of your heart and soul deep into the soil of God's holy ground. Prayer connects you to God so that the life-giving power of his Spirit can flow through you and cause you to bear fruit and glorify his name. Jesus never envisioned his disciples living kingdom lives without significant personal prayer.

Cut the Rope

So what happened to me on that cliff? How did I get out of my suspended mess? I cut my rope. The only way out for me was to hook onto another line that had been dropped down to me and cut the one I had originally used. When I actually put the knife to my rope, I was terrified. After all, at least it was holding me. I had no guarantees about the new rope. But the pain in my legs and my desire to get off that cliff were enough to motivate me to take the risk and cut my line. When I did, I was finally free.

Maybe it's time for you to do some rope cutting. Maybe it's time for you to let go of your secure but unproductive form of Christianity. How would your life look a year from now if you put the knife to your spiritual status quo and prayed every day for God to build his kingdom in your life? How would you live and love differently if you started praying prayers of wild and reckless abandon to God every day? What if, at eighty feet above the rocks, you cut your own lifeline? Would you be free?

Why don't we find out together?

Set Your Faith Free

It's time to start praying for yourself. You're not being selfish when you do. God's Spirit has some work to do in and through you that he can't do without your cooperation. Personal prayer is the beginning point of that process.

In the chapters that follow, I'll show you how to develop the discipline of personal intercession. You'll learn how to find God's promises for your life in his Word. In the next chapter, we'll see how the model of the Lord's Prayer is the perfect place to start when praying for yourself.

In the second part of the book, we'll look at some big, hairy, audacious prayers that every Christian should be praying for himself or herself. When you're finished, even if you're not currently effective in prayer, you'll have several high-impact, biblical prayers to pray for yourself, as well as the equipping and motivation to discover countless others.

In the final part of the book, I'll remind you of some spiritual disciplines that can greatly improve your prayer capacities. They're like performance-enhancing drugs for your soul, only they're legal and highly encouraged by God. When you connect these disciplines with your own prayers, you'll find your prayer life hitting new heights of effectiveness.

Are you ready to take on the discipline of personal intercession? If you do, I can promise that your life will never be the same.

2

Set Your Prayers on Fire

The Power of Pinpoint Praying

This, then, is how you should pray.

Matthew 6:9

The outer court of the Jewish temple in Jerusalem, known as the court of the Gentiles, wasn't typically a quiet or even reverent place. Designed as a place of worship for non-Jews who were seeking to align themselves with the God of the Hebrews, the outer court looked more like a busy marketplace than a place of prayer. Vendors often set up shop right there in the midst of the court and sold animals for sacrifice to those worshipers who had traveled too far to bring their own animals. Buying, selling, bartering, and cheating ran rampant, and, of course, the sounds and smells of sheep, goats, rams, bulls, and pigeons filled the air. Any Gentile seeking to worship in that setting had to be very determined and focused because the environment was anything but conducive to meaningful communion with the holy God.

On one particular day, an unusual and unfamiliar cry rose up among the chants of the buyers and sellers. It was a terrifying, almost animal shriek. It was a battle cry. It was the voice of a man, filled with indignation and rage, which drowned out and eventually silenced the calls of the vendors. Then an amazing sight followed: that man, a well-known religious teacher, made his way through the impromptu marketplace. He yelled at the vendors, turning over their tables, tearing down their makeshift booths, spilling their money, and releasing their animals. In one hand was a whip—an effective instrument of wrath for this indignant messenger.

As the man made his way through the outer courts, his words became more audible, along with the sounds of shouting and chaos that he left behind. This really was a man on a mission. He kept saying, "How dare you! Who do you think you are? What do you think you're doing? This is my Father's house. This is supposed to be a house of prayer. How dare you turn it into a den of thieves! How dare you turn it into a corrupt market!"

You probably know that story. You know that the unlikely vigilante was Jesus, the carpenter-turned-prophet from Nazareth.[1] Have you ever wondered what happened to Jesus on that day? Have you ever thought about what turned the gentle teacher into an enraged warrior? I have a theory. I think it was pinpoint praying.

In John's account of that scene, he noted that as the disciples later reflected on what Jesus had done, they recalled a well-known verse from the Hebrew Scriptures. In Psalm 69, a psalm that most likely pointed to the nature of the promised Messiah, David wrote, "Zeal for your house consumes me"

(v. 9). We already know that as early as age twelve Jesus had identified the temple as his Father's house. We know that he must have developed a sense of his messianic message and mission early in life.

I believe that as Jesus heard certain messianic passages from the Hebrew Scriptures being read or taught, he immediately identified with them. We know that through the reading of Isaiah 61:1–2 he heard God's promise to send an anointed messenger to set captives free. We also know that Jesus realized those holy words were talking about him (see Luke 4:16–21). I believe that when Jesus read or heard such passages, he would pray them for his life. He'd hear the Scriptures speak of a man who would bring hope to the outcasts and healing to the land, and he would pray, "Father, do that in me. Make that true of me."

I believe that when Jesus heard Psalm 69:9, "Zeal for your house consumes me," he began praying that Scripture for himself. He recognized its relevance for his life mission, and he prayed that he would be zealous for and passionate about the house and worship of God. So when Jesus encountered a temple system that was a terrible mockery of the holy place of worship God had designed, all those prayers for zeal and passion kicked in. The result was an act of righteous indignation that was so passionate, pure, and breathtaking that each of the four Gospel writers felt compelled to include it in his account of Jesus's life. What they recorded for us was the fruit of Jesus's pinpoint praying. This is a clear example of what happens when you pray biblically and specifically for your life.

Prayers That Pack a Punch

If you've read any of my *Pray Big* books,[2] then you're probably somewhat familiar with the concept of pinpoint praying. But for those of you who are new to the concept—and even for the rest of us—a review might be helpful.

Pinpoint praying is focused, strategic, powerful praying. It's high-faith, high-impact prayer. The two basic characteristics of pinpoint prayers are that they are biblical and specific. They're biblical because they're based on what God has already promised to do in his Word. They're specific because they ask with pinpoint precision for something very particular and discernable from God. Pinpoint praying is fluff-free, filler-free praying. It goes to the heart of God with biblical accuracy.

Pinpoint praying is the kind of praying that Jesus modeled in his own prayers and the kind that the apostle Paul repeatedly prayed in his letters. Consider some of Jesus's beautiful petitions for the church in John 17:

> Father, glorify the Son that the Son may glorify you (v. 1).
> Holy Father, keep them in your name (v. 11 NASB).
> Keep them from the evil one (v. 15).
> Sanctify them in truth (v. 17).

What do you notice about those prayers? They're pointed, they're powerful, they're brief, and they're consistent with God's will. That's always what you'll find in Jesus's praying, and it's also what you'll find in Paul's.

Paul's epistle to the Ephesians contains some of the most beautiful prayers in the New Testament. In chapter 1, Paul prayed that the believers in Ephesus might have increased wisdom and revelation so they would know God better (see v. 17). He also prayed that they would know the hope, riches, and power that were irreversibly theirs in Christ (see vv. 18–19).

Paul's prayers demonstrate the same pinpoint precision that Jesus's did. They go right to the heart of the matter that he wanted to bring before God. They lack flowery language or a bunch of extra, theologically loaded words. What they do contain are biblical and specific petitions to God, and that's exactly what makes pinpoint praying so effective.

The Greatest Pinpoint Prayer Ever Prayed

In chapter 6 of his Gospel, Matthew records for us what I believe is the greatest example of pinpoint praying offered in the Bible. I'm sure Matthew, one of the original twelve disciples of Jesus, remembered with vivid clarity the moments when Jesus first taught this prayer. On at least two occasions, Jesus taught his disciples how to pray with focus and power. In reality, he was teaching them how to pray pinpoint prayers.

Matthew was in the crowd that day when Jesus preached the greatest sermon in history, the Sermon on the Mount. As one of Jesus's inner crowd, Matthew probably had a ringside seat for that momentous occasion. What Jesus taught that day on that hillside was revolutionary: Blessed are the poor in spirit. Love and pray for your enemies. Hatred is the same as murder, and lust is the same as adultery. When you pray, don't offer up meaningless, repetitive phrases; instead, tell God your needs with biblical precision.

For Jesus, the power of prayer was found in the quality of its words, not its quantity. Here's what Matthew heard Jesus teach that day: "This, then, is how you should pray: 'Our Father in heaven, hallowed be your name, your kingdom come, your will be done on earth as it is in heaven. Give us today our daily bread. Forgive us our debts, as we also have forgiven our debtors. And lead us not into temptation, but deliver us from the evil one'" (Matt. 6:9–13). Never before had so much been said in prayer with so few words. I think the disciples were stunned by Jesus's brevity.

On a different occasion, the disciples asked Jesus about prayer. They had grown up hearing the teachers in the synagogues pray, but when Jesus prayed, they saw prayer on an entirely different level. Luke, probably citing eyewitness accounts, recorded their question: "Lord, teach us to pray" (Luke 11:1). The disciples weren't asking to learn how to pray for the first time. They knew all about prayer. What they didn't know was how to pray like Jesus did. That was what they were seeking. They wanted the authority, the focus, and the power that they no doubt heard in their master's prayers.

So how did Jesus answer them? What did he tell them about effective kingdom praying? Luke recorded Jesus's answer: "When you pray, say: 'Father, hallowed be your name, your kingdom come. Give us each day our daily bread. Forgive us our sins, for we also forgive everyone who sins against us. And lead us not into temptation'" (vv. 2–4).

When I was in college, I had a history professor who used to warn, "If I say something once, write it down. If I say it twice, memorize it. You're going to see it again on a test." So what do you think it means that on two different occasions Jesus offered the same model of prayer for his disciples? It means that in God's kingdom, praying like Jesus is very important. It means that he wants us to pray with the single-mindedness, exactness, authority, and biblical foundation that he modeled for us in these two prayers. It means that prayer is too important for us to load it down with a bunch of meaningless words and repetitive phrases. It means that prayer is how we get things done in God's kingdom. And (don't miss this!) it means that God wants and expects us to pray pinpoint prayers for ourselves.

Five Daily Personal Pinpoint Prayers

The teachings in the Lord's Prayer work great in a group setting or when you're praying for your family, your roommates, or your church. But don't miss the significance of praying these prayers for yourself. Jesus's petitions in the Lord's Prayer are some of the clearest and most direct personal pinpoint prayers ever written.

Based on Jesus's teachings in the Lord's Prayer, here are five pinpoint prayers you can pray for yourself on a daily basis. With just these five prayers, you can address almost every need you'll face on any given day.

Pray for Perspective

Lord, let your name be hallowed in my life today.

The significance of how Jesus opened this prayer is difficult to overstate. Rather than telling us to approach God first with our needs, Jesus instructs us to seek the proper perspective on them. What we need most on a daily basis is for God's name to be treated as holy (hallowed) in our lives.

This is a humbling prayer. It reminds us that the world does not revolve around us. A local cable provider in my city runs an ad that goes something like this: "You want the meeting to start when you get there. You want the bus to leave when you're ready. You want to catch your favorite shows when it's convenient for you. You want to watch the game on your schedule. Basically, you're at the center of your universe. We like the way you think!" If we listen to enough of that kind of reasoning, it's easy to start thinking that it's true. That's why we need to begin every day praying for God's name to be hallowed. It reminds us who the universe really does revolve around (so to speak), and who it doesn't. It helps us remember that there is nothing in our lives as important as the holiness and glory of God.

When you're battling with your flesh to keep the proper perspective, this is a great prayer to pray. Ask God for this attitude and mind-set every day. Pray Psalm 115:1 for yourself: *Lord, not to me, but to your name be the glory.*

Pray for Priorities

Lord, let your kingdom be established and your will be done in my life today.

As Jesus continued his prayer, he still didn't turn to the point of asking about personal needs and wants. There was one more area he wanted us to address first in prayer.

To pray for God's kingdom to be built in your life is to ask for God's rule and reign to have its perfect way in you. You're acknowledging that your heart and soul are God's throne, and you're inviting him to reign there. To pray for God's will is to surrender to God's plan for your life and to confess that you trust his judgment over your own. It's to welcome God's course and curriculum for your life, no matter how difficult or painful.

When you pray this prayer, you're praying that your words, attitudes, actions, spending habits, relationships, work ethic, recreation, and spare time would all be places where God's rule is welcome. You're totally yielding every aspect of your life to God.

Can you see the significance of praying this prayer for yourself at the beginning of every day? Seeking God's kingdom and his will for your life through prayer helps to set the thermostat of your heart on high when it comes to the things of God. It removes your right or expectation for negotiation with God on matters of obedience. And it makes you a pliable and usable tool in God's hands.

Pray for God's priorities to be worked out in your life. Pray Matthew 6:33 and 6:10 for yourself: *Lord, as I seek your kingdom and your righteousness, please be enthroned in my life.*

Pray for Provision

Lord, please give me everything I need today.

The prayer for "daily bread" is one of the most liberating, radical prayers a Christ-follower can pray. When you pray for God to give you your daily bread, you're totally recalibrating your heart and mind to God's definition of provision. This pinpoint prayer blows up any sense of entitlement you may have. It puts your financial world in the proper perspective.

As I write these words, the church I pastor is facing a mild financial shortfall. We are coming off a year when our church members gave $400,000 over our budget. But this year our giving has been flat, especially in light of the fact that we're still a rapidly growing church. The bean counters in our accounting office tell me that in just two months, we'll be down to $200,000 in our savings account. Given that our budget is over $7 million, that's not much for "rainy day" savings. But when I read what Jesus taught about praying for provision, I have a difficult time feeling too concerned. That $200,000 we have in savings is exactly $200,000 *more* than Jesus promised us. He promised to meet our needs today.

Honestly, I can't think of a single thing that our church needs today that we don't have. I can think of lots of things we want and some things we're going to need, but there's nothing that we need *today* that Jesus hasn't already given us. That's what he promised.

When you pray for God to provide for your daily needs, you help to boost your contentment levels. Discontentedness is at the root of things such as greed and covetousness, both of which are disastrous to your relationship with God. But by praying for simple daily provision, you acknowledge that you don't need much. You acknowledge that God's love, mercy, and presence are more important to you than material things.

Learn to pray for your daily bread. Pray to be content with what you have. Pray 1 Timothy 6:8 for yourself: *Lord, if I have food and clothing, I will be content with that.*

Pray for Pardon

Lord, please forgive me today.

On Super Bowl Sunday in 1995, seventeen-year-old Brandon Blendon climbed into his pickup and went for a drive after the game. He had an open can of beer propped between his legs and two more in his front seat. At an intersection, Brandon rear-ended a car that had stopped for a red light. The impact killed a four-year-old girl who had been secured in her safety seat in the backseat of the car.

A judge sentenced Brandon to twenty years in prison and ordered him to pay $520 in restitution to the little girl's parents. Each week for ten years, Brandon has to mail a check for one dollar to the family, with a note in the memo line reading, "For causing the death of your daughter Whitney!" While Whitney's mom has forgiven Brandon and even visits him in prison, Brandon will never be able to escape the reality of what he did. He has an ugly, weekly reminder of what his sin cost not only him but several other innocent people as well.[3]

Too many Christians live with terrible guilt because of mistakes made years, even decades, before. They live in the shadow of what they've done, not of who they are in Christ. In essence they write checks to God in some unhealthy effort to remind themselves of their mistakes and how bad they are. That's not what God wants. He sent Christ to the cross to free us from our past, not chain us to it. Seeking God's forgiveness in our daily prayers helps us keep our slates clean before God. It makes our yokes easy and our burdens light, which is exactly what Jesus offered (see Matt. 11:28–30).

Forgiveness is a powerful thing. It has the ability to transform a person's life and shatter years of guilt and shame. It is one of the most freeing, life-giving gifts a person can receive or give. That's why Jesus commanded us in his prayer both to seek forgiveness from God and to extend it to others. Forgiveness was important enough to Jesus to include it in his daily plan for pinpoint praying for our lives.

When you seek forgiveness from God, you're acknowledging that there are still things—thoughts, habits, actions, inactions, and attitudes—that are inconsistent with the call to be holy that God has placed on your life. Your prayer for forgiveness keeps your relationship with God fresh and vibrant.

When you forgive others in prayer, you're also acknowledging the equal footing we all have as desperate sinners before God. Failing to forgive others is sin for us, as it sets us up as a god over someone else. Jesus's command to forgive here is based on simple, kingdom logic: if God, who is holy and infinite, chooses to forgive us, then we who are unholy and finite must forgive as well. To not forgive makes us less forgiving than God.

In your daily prayers, be sure to pray for forgiveness from God and to forgive others. It will keep your relational world healthy and will keep you in a humble posture before God. Pray Colossians 3:13 for yourself: *Father, please help me to bear with other people's faults and to quickly forgive whatever grievances I may have against anyone. Help me to forgive as you forgave me.*

33

Pray for Protection

Lord, please keep me from Satan and sin today.

I find it very intriguing that Jesus ended his prayer with an appeal for spiritual protection and deliverance. No person better understood the real nature of the battle between good and evil in our world than Jesus. But the good and evil that he knew of weren't impersonal forces that blindly oppose each other and haphazardly influence people. Jesus didn't believe in yin and yang, and he wasn't talking about karma. Jesus believed in the devil. He'd fought him firsthand, so he spoke of his power from experience. Jesus felt that the threat of Satan to the lives of believers was significant enough to merit daily pinpoint praying against it.

When you pray for freedom from temptation and deliverance from evil (literally, "the evil one"), you're asking God to help you spiritually discern the opportunities for failure that you face every day. Good spiritual discernment will help you not only to recognize temptation for what it is but also to recognize Satan's ultimate goal in the temptation. Jesus taught that Satan wants to kill, steal, and destroy (see John 10:10). We need to keep that in mind when flirting with temptations that look benign on the surface.

This pinpoint prayer for protection asks God to allow only the temptations and tests in your life that will grow you and glorify him. Were Satan permitted to throw all of his dark powers against you, there would be no chance of your standing up against him. But by praying for spiritual protection, you ask God to put a cap on the degree to which Satan can harass and attack you. God actually uses his archenemy's evil schemes to develop you, but he only allows the degree of temptation that you can successfully withstand and grow through (see 1 Cor. 10:13).

You can't go through your life free from temptation and satanic attack, but you can go through it victoriously. You don't have to be a spiritual punching bag for the devil. Pray for protection. Pray Romans 16:19–20 for your life: *Lord Jesus, make me wise about what is good and innocent about what is evil. I pray that you, the God of peace, would soon crush Satan under my feet.*

Set Your Faith Free

How would your life look different if you prayed these simple pinpoint prayers for yourself every day? When Jesus gave us these potent prayers, he wasn't looking for sermon filler. Jesus believed and taught that if we would pray these requests for our lives, we would find ourselves living in the middle of God's will and honoring his kingdom. So here's a question: can you afford *not* to pray these prayers?

In Ephesians 6, Paul urged the believers in Ephesus to put on the whole spiritual armor of God (see vv. 10–17). Paul didn't hesitate to pray for God's daily covering for his life, and neither should we. Become a personal intercessor. Start seeking God's perspective, priorities, provision, pardon, and protection for your daily life. Be sure to keep a prayer journal. You won't believe how different your life will look in just a few months!

3

Finding Buried Treasure

Mining God's Word for Pinpoint Promises

Your word is a lamp to my feet and a light for my path.

Psalm 119:105

I n 2007 Willie Joe Wright, Cynthia Wright's husband of many years, died suddenly and tragically during heart surgery. Cynthia was devastated. After Willie Joe's funeral, Cynthia took his Bible (he had been a strong Christian and a deacon in their church), as well as several other sentimental keepsakes, and set them on a shelf in the garage of their home in West Palm Beach, Florida.

On a Thursday morning in March 2008, Cynthia left her house earlier than usual to take her granddaughter to her ballet lesson. Not fifteen minutes later, she got a call from a panicked neighbor telling her that her house was engulfed in flames. By the time she got back to her home, it was gone. Everything had been taken by the flames—everything, that is, except Willie Joe's Bible. According to police reports, the fire burned the cover off the Bible, leaving it open to a picture of Jesus. The firefighters who worked at the scene were so moved by the Bible's miraculous survival that they took a picture of it amid the charred ruins and asked Cynthia for permission to hang it in their firehouse. In the picture, the bright, colorful image of Jesus stands out in vivid contrast to the charred ruins around it. Cynthia knows that God was sending her a message by allowing the Bible to survive. She knows that no matter what happens to her—whether it be the loss of her life partner or a devastating house fire—God is going to be looking out for her. She has his Word on it.[1]

Standing on the Promises

When it comes to surviving the fires of life, the Bible really does offer the best hope and inspiration. When it comes to navigating through the storms of life, the Bible really does provide the best instruction and guidance. And when it comes to knowing how to pray for ourselves and others, the Bible really is the best prayer script.

King David knew all about the power of God's Word for guiding him through life. Over a thousand years before Christ, he wrote:

> How can a young man keep his way pure? By living according to your word.
>
> Psalm 119:9

My soul is weary with sorrow; strengthen me according to your word.

verse 28

I have more insight than all my teachers, for I meditate on your statutes.

verse 99

Your word is a lamp to my feet and a light for my path.

verse 105

It would have been difficult for David to overstate the importance of God's Word in his life. And remember, David didn't have a Bible. He had the law of Moses and some of the early recorded history of Israel. But he didn't have the fully revealed Word of God or the Holy Spirit living in him and teaching him about what God had said. And yet David still knew that the best guide for his daily life, thoughts, and prayers was God's Word.

What was true for David is even truer for us. We have the complete Old and New Testaments. We know the promises to Israel through the prophets and the hope for sinners given through Christ. We know that God has opened up his family to all people—Gentiles and Jews—who believe in his Son. We also have the Holy Spirit living in us. He's teaching, guiding, and praying for us all the time. And the number one tool the Spirit uses for his work in us is God's Word.

If you're looking for the best available resource to add fuel to prayers for your life, then look no further than the Bible. It's all you need. In the remainder of this chapter, you'll learn how to read the Bible not just for content's sake but as a guide for your praying. In the next few pages, you're going to learn how to mine God's Word for his endless and priceless promises for your life.

Bible Mining 101

You don't have to be a Bible scholar to pray God's Word effectively. In fact, all you need is the simple, childlike faith that God really will speak to you through the Scriptures, as well as a system that gets you in the pages of the Bible on a regular basis.

Here are a few suggestions for making reading and praying the Bible a regular part of your life. They represent the system I've used since the early 1990s, but they're not inspired. Don't be legalistic or rigid with them. Use them as guidelines. The more time you spend with God in his Word, the more you'll begin to discover your own system for mining its treasures.

Have a regular time for prayer. If you delay your daily praying until you have time for it, it won't happen. Prayer needs to be as important in your routine as eating, sleeping, and personal hygiene. Set a time to meet with God—five minutes, ten minutes, fifteen minutes, whatever—and then be ruthless about protecting it.

I read and pray in the morning. I'm able to guard my calendar, so I rarely schedule anything that might keep me from having my early prayer time. Occasionally, when I've had a particularly hard day and need some extra prayer, I'll throw in another few minutes at night.

There's no right or wrong time for prayer. Do what works best for you. Just be faithful to pray every day. That's the point.

Have a regular place for prayer. If possible, have a specific place where you meet with God. It could be at your kitchen table with a hot cup of coffee, in a cozy chair in your living room, or at an office desk. But when it comes to prayer, familiarity breeds intimacy. You don't want new sights, sounds, and settings distracting you from your conversation with God. As much as possible, you want your place of prayer to be protected and free from interruptions.

Give yourself some grace on this one. You're not always going to be able to have interruption-free times of prayer. Phones are going to ring; delivery men are going to knock on your door; babies are going to cry; and children, spouses, or roommates are going to demand your attention. Be patient with them and trust that God won't check out, even if you have to for a few minutes.

Have a regular system for prayer. I believe that it's good to know in advance where you're going to read in the Bible. The sixty-six books of the Bible offer countless pinpoint prayers that we can be praying for ourselves and our loved ones. If you can, try to have a reading plan that gets you all the way through the Bible in a year. But don't force it. Be open to the Spirit's guidance on what to read.

I read from two different Bible translations in my prayer times, and I read different sections of the Bible in each of those translations. I try to read through the Bible at least once a year, if not more frequently. That works for me, but do what's best for you.

I also read and pray through part of the Psalms every day. I have found the book of Psalms to be my best source for pinpoint prayers, so I typically pray through a few chapters of it each day. When I finish the last chapter, Psalm 150, I just put my bookmark back on Psalm 1 so I can start over the next day. Praying the Psalms never gets old. My life and the lives of those I love have been greatly impacted because of the powerful pinpoint prayers I've been able to pray from the Psalms.

When you read the Bible, look for statements of what you want to be true in your life. This is the most important part of finding pinpoint prayers in the Bible. You have to read with your spiritual eyes open. As you read through the verses of a particular chapter, don't be in a hurry. The goal is not just to get to the end. You're looking for treasure. You're looking for verses that jump off the page. You're looking for promises that connect with your passions.

As you read, listen for the gentle nudge of God's Holy Spirit. Ask him to speak to you through the text. Occasionally you'll hear him say, "I want to do this in you," or, "You need to pray this verse for your life." When you sense that leading about a particular verse, you've just discovered one of your very own pinpoint promises. So right then, stop and write your initials next to that verse. Then, every time you read that chapter or open your Bible to that page, you'll be reminded to pray God's Word back to him. You'll be reminded to ask God to do in you what his Word says.

Let me give you an example. This morning, in my own prayer time, I was reading through Psalm 91 in the New International Version. As I was reading and trying to listen to God's Spirit, verse 15 hit me particularly hard. It says, "He will call upon me, and I will answer him; I will be with him in trouble, I will deliver him and honor him." Immediately I wanted to start praying that verse for my life. I'm in a season right now where I really need my prayers to be focused and pointed before God. I desperately need to know that God hears me, that he will answer me, and that he will protect me in times of trouble. I'm not so concerned about the "honor" part, but I would be thrilled if God would honor his name through me.

I took my pen and wrote my initials (WDD) next to that verse in my Bible. Now, whenever I read Psalm 91, I'll be reminded to ask God to hear me, to answer me, and to be with me in trouble. I'll remember the particular season in my life when I needed assurance that God heard my prayers, and when he gently whispered to me through some three-thousand-year-old words that he did.

In my Bible, I have literally hundreds of verses marked with the initials of my wife and kids, my church, my hometown, and our country. My Bible has become more than my prayer guide; it's my prayer script. I never have to worry about what I'm going to say to God about a certain subject. The answer is always right there in his Word.

When Does a Verse Become a Promise?

People often ask me, "How do I know when it's okay to pray a verse for myself? How do I know I'm not being greedy or self-centered? How can I be sure that I'm really hearing the Spirit, and it's not just my own wishful thinking?"

In Deuteronomy 28 God gave some tremendous promises to Israel. If they stayed faithful to him, he said:

> The LORD will open the heavens, the storehouse of his bounty, to send rain on your land in season and to bless all the work of your hands. You will lend to many nations but will borrow from none. The LORD will make you the head, not the tail. If you pay attention to the commands of the LORD your God that I give you this day and carefully follow them, you will always be at the top, never at the bottom.
>
> Deuteronomy 28:12–13

It would be very easy to read those wonderful promises and want them to be true of you. I'm sure you would love to have God bless you with his rich bounty. Of course, you'd prefer to be financially secure and to be in a position to lend instead of borrow. You'd probably rather be at the front of the pack, not at the back, and to be the head, not the tail. Who wouldn't?

42

But can any of us really pray those verses for our lives without being selfish or greedy? How do we know those promises are really pinpoint prayers that God wants us to pray for our lives?

Discovering pinpoint prayers isn't an exact science. You're going to have to learn to discern the Spirit's voice and to approach God's Word humbly. The following are some questions you can ask as you try to distinguish between God's promptings about a promise for your life and your own desires and wants.

Will this honor God? This is a great first question to ask before you start praying a verse for yourself. The Holy Spirit's job is to honor and exalt God, not us. We're to point others to him, not ourselves. If you can pray a verse with God's glory in mind, then you're probably on safe ground biblically.

What's my motivation for wanting this? If you're asking God to give you the wealth of Abraham or the fame of Solomon, what's your reasoning? Why do you want riches? Is it so you can funnel more resources to God's work, or is it so you can live a cushy life? And why are you seeking fame? Do you want popularity and fans? Or are you seeking a platform from which to proclaim God's Word? Your true motives will tell you a lot about whether or not you've really heard God in a verse. Do an honest gut check if you're not sure.

Is this consistent with what the Bible as a whole teaches? It's easy to read a verse and forget to consider it in light of its biblical context. Finding pinpoint promises in the Bible certainly requires you to listen for God to speak to you through specific verses, but it also requires you to use good biblical interpretation skills. Here's a good rule of thumb: if what you think the verse promises is inconsistent with the whole of biblical teaching, then you're probably not hearing God. God will not lead you to contradict his Word. So if you're not sure that what you're praying is biblical, check it out in light of the overall teaching of Scripture. If you're uncertain, ask someone who knows the Bible better than you do.

Here are a few examples of the Bible being misunderstood and misused in prayer for unbiblical things:

- A man hoping to find justification for his affair read about King David's affair with Bathsheba. He used David's desire for and subsequent tryst with the married Bathsheba as biblical justification for his own adulterous behavior.

- In Malachi 3:10, God promised to open the windows of heaven and pour out blessing in response to his people's faithful tithing. Many people have used those words to pray for and expect worldly wealth as part of the gospel's promise. While God clearly honors giving, the promise of material wealth is nowhere connected to the gospel message in the New Testament.

- Some people have used God's Old Testament commands to destroy entire groups of people as justification for praying for and promoting physical violence against God's "enemies," such as doctors who perform abortions. Such prayers are completely inconsistent with God's prohibition against murder and Jesus's command to love and pray for our enemies.

In each of those extreme examples, the verses in question were not viewed in light of the whole of biblical teaching. God wants us to scour his Word in search of pinpoint promises, but he expects us to be biblically responsible in the process. We don't have permission to misappropriate God's Word for the sake of our own selfish or sinful preferences. God won't reward, but rather will judge, such misuse of his Word.

Would Jesus himself pray for this? This may be the best question to ask when discerning the appropriateness of a pinpoint prayer. Simply ask yourself, *Would Jesus agree with this prayer? Would he put his seal of approval on it?* In John 14:13–14, Jesus encouraged us to ask for things in his name. But the phrase "in Jesus's name" that we use in prayer isn't just a rote expression we tack on to the end of our requests. Praying in Jesus's name means that we are praying for something that Jesus himself would pray for. It means that our requests are consistent with the heart, passion, and mission of Jesus and are in agreement with the kingdom-building work of the Holy Spirit.

As I feel led to pray a verse for my life, marriage, ministry, or family, I always pause to see if I can biblically and confidently say that prayer in Jesus's name. Am I sure that Jesus would agree with me on it? If I'm not, then I typically rethink what God might be saying to me in the verse. You can do the same. Be mature and responsible enough to run your pinpoint prayers through the "in Jesus's name" filter.

Set Your Faith Free

Praying for yourself doesn't have to be difficult. It can be almost as natural as breathing. If you can pray, "Lord, do that in me," then you can become an effective self-intercessor. Start today using God's Word as your prayer script. If you don't know where to start, try Psalm 1. Don't just read it; pray through it. My guess is that you'll find two or three verses that will prompt you to confidently say, "Lord, do that in me," or, "Lord, let that be true of me." When you do, God's Spirit will say, "Amen," and Jesus will also say, "Amen. I agree." And then you'll find that you're slowly changing, as God does exactly what you've asked and what his Word promises.[2]

Part 2

Pinpoint Prayers
for Yourself

I urge you, brothers, by our Lord Jesus Christ and
by the love of the Spirit, to join me in my struggle
by praying to God for me.

Romans 15:30

In this part, I'll share several pinpoint prayers that I pray
for myself almost every day. They're certainly not the only
ones I pray for myself, but they're some of the most important
ones. I've been praying them for years.

My purpose here is twofold. First, I want to provide some
good starter prayers for you. You can easily pray these same
prayers for yourself. They're broad enough and universal
enough that just about everyone can relate to them. Sec-

ond, and more importantly, I want to spur your thinking about your own pinpoint prayers. I hope that as you see how I pray for myself, the Holy Spirit will begin to lead you to ideas and Scriptures that will become your own personal pinpoint prayers.

4

Arm in Arm with Jesus

Prayers for Proximity

When they saw the courage of Peter and John
and realized that they were unschooled, ordinary
men, they were astonished and they took note that
these men had been with Jesus.

Acts 4:13

Not long ago, my wife and I went to hear a visiting
violinist play with the Austin Chamber Orchestra.
They were performing Vivaldi's *Four Seasons*. Now, you need
to understand that I'm much more likely to be seen at a Doo-
bie Brothers concert than a classical music concert, but I
do sometimes have moments of civility, and this was one of
them. Besides, Susie made me go.

The performance was amazing. The violinist was quite
good, and he brought to life the beauty and intricacies of

Vivaldi's great work. At one point in the concert, the violinist was playing a long solo. The members of the orchestra sat quietly behind him as he played, watching their scores and following what he was doing. Suddenly I noticed that many of the orchestra members started smiling and even giggling among themselves. Obviously the soloist had done something they thought was funny. He didn't miss any notes—at least not any that my untrained ear could discern. But somewhere along the way he had added a measure or skipped a few bars or did something that the musicians behind him thought was funny. It was obviously an inside joke.

That drove me crazy. I wanted to know what I had missed. I had to resist the urge to stand up and yell, "Hey, wait a minute. What just happened? What's so funny? Could you please let the rest of us in on the secret?" What impressed me, and even made me a little jealous, was the way the rest of the musicians synced with the soloist. They obviously knew him and the music well enough to sense even the most subtle changes. When he did something, they were right there with him.

That's how you want to be with Jesus. You want to be so close, so tightly connected, so familiar with his ways, that when he moves or speaks or nudges, you immediately sense it. You don't want any distance between you and Jesus. That's why you should pray for proximity to him. Pray that wherever he is, you'll be there too. Pray that you'll know his ways and always be right at his side.

Deadly Distance

Following Jesus at a distance can be very dangerous. When you're at the back of the pack, it's easy to get picked off by the enemy. The safest place to be is right next to Jesus.

50

The disciple Peter learned this lesson the hard way. On the night Jesus was arrested, Peter had gone out of his way to declare his loyalty to Jesus. He made the bold claim in front of the rest of the disciples that he was ready to die for Jesus. But later, after Jesus had been arrested and Peter had taken off a soldier's ear with a wild swing of his sword, he lost some of his nerve. He didn't abandon Jesus entirely, but he didn't stay at Jesus's side either.

Luke describes what happened: "Then seizing him [Jesus], they led him away and took him into the house of the high priest. Peter followed *at a distance*" (Luke 22:54, emphasis added). It was that "distance" that would get Peter into serious trouble. Peter was too far away from Christ to be easily identified as a disciple. Within the hour, he would deny three times that he even knew Jesus. What a long fall for Peter. In just a matter of hours he went from swearing his allegiance to Jesus and risking his life for him, to swearing that he didn't know him. What was the difference? Proximity.

It's never a good idea to put distance between you and Jesus. If you do, you just might end up falling as Peter did. So pray for your relationship with Christ. Pray that you will always be near him. Pray that there would be no distance between you.

Just a Closer Walk with Thee

When Jesus called his disciples, he made them an unusual offer. Mark tells us that Jesus "appointed twelve—designating them apostles—that they might *be with him*" (Mark 3:14, emphasis added). Part of Jesus's invitation to his disciples was just to spend time with him. He wasn't looking for mere workers; he wanted brothers. He wanted men he could pour himself into and reproduce in his image.

His unconventional strategy paid off. Years later, after Jesus had ascended into heaven, Peter and John were confronted by the same tribunal that had condemned Jesus. Luke tells us, "When they [the members of the tribunal] saw the courage of Peter and John and realized that they were unschooled, ordinary men, they were astonished and they took note that these men had *been with Jesus*" (Acts 4:13, emphasis added). There was something strange, almost eerily familiar about the men who were proclaiming Christ. Finally the members of the tribunal made the connection: these same men had walked with, trained with, and lived with Jesus.

Do you see the obvious difference in Peter from the night he denied Christ? When he followed Jesus at a distance, he was quick to fall. But later, when he crossed over the line of radical obedience and forever closed the distance between himself and Christ, he became a bold disciple. That's what proximity does. The closer you are to Jesus—the more you walk with him and the less distance you allow between you—the easier it is to live for him.

The Secret to Proximity

In John 15, Jesus gave his disciples a vivid picture of what it means to be close to him. It was the night before his crucifixion, and Jesus wanted to make sure his followers knew the secret to staying near him in the tumultuous days and years that lay ahead. Here's part of what he told them: "Remain in me, and I will remain in you. No branch can bear fruit by itself; it must remain in the vine. Neither can you bear fruit unless you remain in me" (v. 4).

Jesus used the familiar imagery of a vineyard to help his disciples see the importance of staying connected to him. They lived in an agrarian world, and it was easy for them to make the association between fruit bearing and abiding. Branches that are cut off from the vine stop yielding fruit and quickly die, and Jesus wanted his disciples to understand that the same was true for them: as long as they remained in close proximity to him, they'd be fruitful, but if they allowed distance to creep into their relationship, they were in big trouble. It's tragic that Peter, only a few hours after hearing Jesus give this warning, became a graphic example of how quickly the lack of proximity can seriously damage a disciple.

A Christ-follower who abides or remains in Christ never does so by accident. Staying connected to Jesus requires focus, discipline, and intention. I believe that, without exception, the most important ingredient in staying close to Jesus is God's Word. Twice in his teaching on fruit bearing, Jesus mentioned the importance of God's Word (see John 15:3, 7). The Bible, very much like the vine in Jesus's metaphor, provides the life-giving nutrients that make us fruitful. Christians who live off a steady diet of God's Word will find it much easier to remain in Christ and bear fruit than those who neglect the regular reading and study of Scripture.

Pray for a hunger for God's Word. Pray for your spiritual proximity to Christ and for a closeness to his Word. Pray that you'll love and be hungry for the truths of Scripture.[1] Then act on your prayers and start reading God's Word every day. The steady diet of Scripture will go a long way toward helping you remain true to Christ and keeping you from slipping back into the shadows.

Arm in Arm with Jesus

Below is an image you can use for inspiration as you pray for your proximity to Jesus. It inspires me as I pray for my own

53

walk with Christ. It's from the film *The Passion of the Christ* and based on the scene described in Matthew 27:32.

As Jesus makes his way to Golgotha, the place where he is to be crucified, he is too weak and bloodied to carry his cross alone. The Roman soldiers grab a man from the crowd, Simon of Cyrene, and force him to help Jesus carry his cross. In one powerful scene, Jesus falls to the ground and can't go on. A mob immediately begins to beat him. Simon, who is rapidly developing an affinity for Christ, comes to his rescue. He beats back the crowd and then begins screaming at the Roman soldiers. He tells them that he doesn't care what they do to him, but if they don't stop harassing Jesus, he won't carry the cross any further.

Then Simon stoops down and helps Jesus pick up his cross. We see the two men from behind as they slowly stand up together. They move side by side, each with an arm over the other man's shoulder. The cross is between them.

The view from that angle lasted only for a moment, but it immediately grabbed my attention, and I have never forgotten it: Jesus's arm, bloodied and bruised, is interlocked with Simon's, and together they carry Jesus's cross.

I want that image to represent my walk with Christ. I want to be that close to Jesus, that close to his cross. I want to get his blood all over me. I don't want to shy away from any shame or persecution that might come through affiliation with him. And when he is mocked, I want to rush quickly to his defense. I don't want to care what happens to me, as long as Jesus is exalted.

Set Your Faith Free

Pray that you will have a heart like Simon's. Pray that you will always be arm in arm with Jesus. Ask God to keep

54

you close to his Son and never allow you to drift into the shadows. Pray that you'll remain faithfully at Jesus's side, safe in his loving protection and boldly identifying yourself as his disciple. Pray Luke 9:23 for yourself: *Lord Jesus, help me to want to follow you. Give me grace each day to deny myself, to identify with you and the glorious cause of your cross, and to follow you.*

5

No Delay

Prayers for Your Obedience Response Time

Whoever has my commands and obeys them,
he is the one who loves me. He who loves me
will be loved by my Father, and I too will love
him and show myself to him.

John 14:21

When God says "Go," how long does it take you to respond? Are you prone to negotiate, stall, or seek second and third opinions? Do you look for escape clauses and pre-obedience agreements? Or, when God speaks, do you respond immediately?

If you are a parent, you probably don't put up with delayed obedience from your children. You teach them to trust your judgment, to respect your authority, and to do what you tell them to do immediately and without any stalling. God expects the same from you. He expects you to trust him, to honor him, and to obey him. He promises to bless and reward you when you do. Pray for your obedience response time (ORT) to grow shorter and shorter. Pray that when you hear God's command, you will obey instantly.

World-Class Obedience

The Bible is loaded with examples of men and women who practiced instant obedience. Consider Noah, who obeyed God and started construction on an ark even though the concept of a flood was probably foreign to him. God honored his obedience and preserved him and his family through the most terrible days the world had ever seen. Consider Abraham, who obeyed God and left his hometown in search of a far country he had never seen but God had promised to give him. God honored his obedience and made him the father of Israel.

In my opinion, Abraham also received one of the most difficult assignments God ever gave a human. Without any explanation, God commanded Abraham to offer his beloved and promised son, Isaac, as a sacrifice to him. The biblical text records Abraham's radical response to God's brutal assignment: "Early the next morning Abraham got up and saddled his donkey. He took with him two of his servants and his son Isaac. When he had cut enough wood for the burnt offering, he set out for the place God had told him about" (Gen. 22:3). I'm stunned and humbled by Abraham's unblinking response to God. We know from the text that Abraham was fully prepared to carry out God's difficult order, even though he didn't fully understand God's reasoning. He did, however, know that God is good and that he could be trusted, even with the life of his promised son. God honored Abraham's faith.

In the New Testament, Jesus's first disciples also demonstrated impressively short ORTs. The writer Mark tells us that when Jesus approached Simon and Andrew and invited them to join his ministry, "at once they left their nets and followed him" (Mark 1:18). That was probably not the first time Simon and Andrew had met Jesus. They were aware of his ministry and his rising popularity. But it was probably the first time Jesus had extended his call and command on their lives, and their response to him was instant—no negotiation, no debating, no stalling; just an immediate yes to the call of the Lord.

We need to pray for equally obedient hearts. We need to pray that when Jesus calls, we'll drop our nets and follow.

Starbucks and Blankets

Tony Colvin is currently the director of creative arts at the church I pastor. Tony and his wife, Karen, are two of my favorite people, and they have always demonstrated a high degree of commitment to doing God's will, no matter how challenging. Tony left a higher-paying, solid sales career at Dell to come work for our church. Tony has a very short ORT.

Tony was at home one night getting ready for bed when he felt the Holy Spirit nudging him to do something. As he sat quietly and listened to the Lord, he sensed that God wanted him to minister to someone right then—that night—before he went to bed. Think about how easy it would have been for Tony to write off such a leading as too inconvenient or too radical to be obeyed right then. But Tony really felt as if the Spirit was telling him that someone needed care that night—obeying early the next morning wouldn't be good enough.

Tony got dressed, told his wife he was going out, and then drove to a nearby Starbucks to pick up some coffee to go. Then he picked up a bag of cheeseburgers and just started driving, praying for the Holy Spirit to lead him. After a few minutes, Tony noticed a man with a backpack crossing a dark intersection into a highway department storage yard. Tony had found his mission. He got out of his car, walked right into the area where he had seen the man, and called out to him, asking if he was hungry or wanted some coffee. The man warmly received both Tony and the hot coffee. Tony stayed longer than he had originally intended that night and even took the man to Walmart to purchase a new jacket and blanket. When he left the area, which turned out to be a homeless camp, he did so with a great sense of fulfillment and joy. He knew he had done what God wanted him to do and that God wasn't finished with him.

Tony developed a relationship with the people at the camp, and he learned their names and most of their stories. He and some other people from our church have provided them with blankets, clothing, food, and even tents. In some cases, Tony arranged for them to work at our church in return for such things as bus tickets or help with rent.

Tony learned that ministry to the homeless is messy—not just physically, but emotionally and spiritually. They are not the easiest people in the world to minister to, but they matter to Jesus, and therefore they have to matter to Jesus's people. Tony knows that his obedience that night brought both immediate and long-term blessing to the lives of some people who desperately needed it. He also knows that it has forever changed him.

It has changed our church as well. Because of Tony's obedience, we are developing a homeless ministry. We're learning about the most effective ways to help homeless people, and we're connecting with other ministries in the city who can help us make wise decisions as we try to serve our new friends.

Some of the homeless are starting to contribute to our church too. They built a backdrop and set that we used for a vision series. The set included a homeless camp with items they had "donated." And recently, at our Easter weekend services, two of the homeless came and helped set up beforehand. Then they stayed and worshiped with us. Tony later commented that seeing his two homeless friends there, singing and raising their hands in worship along with the well-dressed congregation that crowded into our church that weekend, was one of the coolest and most meaningful things he's ever seen.

Why Pray for Instant Obedience?

There are several reasons to pray for a rapid obedience response time. Here are just a few.

First, God promises to honor obedience. The Bible is loaded with statements about the importance of obedience in a believer's life. God seems to go out of his way to make the case for the benefits of obedience. That is something that he didn't have to do, by the way. He could require our obedience just because it's right and he's God. He could expect us to follow his Word and not give any promise of blessing or benefit for it. But that's not how God operates. He's a loving, benevolent God who honors the obedience of his people.

Listen to some of God's promises to the nation of Israel regarding obedience:

> If you fully obey the LORD your God and carefully follow all his commands I give you today, the LORD your God will set you high above all the nations on earth. All these blessings will come upon you and accompany you if you obey the LORD your God:
>
> You will be blessed in the city and blessed in the country.
>
> The fruit of your womb will be blessed, and the crops of your land and the young of your livestock—the calves of your herds and the lambs of your flocks.
>
> Your basket and your kneading trough will be blessed.
>
> You will be blessed when you come in and blessed when you go out.
>
> The LORD will grant that the enemies who rise up against you will be defeated before you. They will come at you from one direction but flee from you in seven.
>
> The LORD will send a blessing on your barns and on everything you put your hand to. The LORD your God will bless you in the land he is giving you.
>
> The LORD will establish you as his holy people, as he promised you on oath, if you keep the commands of the LORD your God and walk in his ways. Then all the peoples on earth will see that you are called by the name of the LORD, and they will fear you.
>
> Deuteronomy 28:1–10

It would be difficult to overstate the abundance of favor that God promises to show to those who obey him. I don't know what exactly those great promises (and the countless others like them in the Bible) mean for the lives of believers today, but I do know that God is faithful to his Word. That's why I always tell Christians who are wrestling with their ORT that God honors obedience. If you are faithful to him, he promises to be even more faithful to you. His Word promises it.

Second, obedience increases your spiritual maturity. When God calls you to a step of obedience, there is always more going on than what you can immediately see or discern. God may indeed want you to serve a neighbor, forgive an enemy, or repent of a sin, but he typically is also working another, longer-term agenda. When God calls you to obey him, he wants to mature you.

Radical obedience is a crash course in spiritual maturity. When you step out in obedience to God's call, you guarantee that your maturity will increase and your walk with him will deepen. Besides bringing God's favor and blessing, obedience brings depth to the most important relationship you have— your relationship with God.

When Moses accepted God's call to lead the Israelites out of Egypt, he entered into an adventure of growth and intimacy with God that lasted eighty years. Moses discovered things about God that he would never have known had he remained in the safety of the Sinai Desert. When Peter stepped out of the boat onto the stormy waters of the Sea of Galilee, he too entered into a level of relational intimacy with Jesus that he wouldn't have known otherwise. And even though he lost his courage and quickly began to sink, he still experienced something with Jesus that the others in the boat missed.

Instant obedience thrusts you into a level of dependence on and knowledge of Christ that is impossible to realize in the supposedly safe quarters of sluggish obedience. Pray for an immediate ORT, because your spiritual development depends on it. You'll never become what God intends you to be as long as you argue and negotiate with him when he calls. Get up and get going; step out of the boat. You can't afford not to.

Finally, your instant obedience causes a ripple effect of blessing. The impact of obedience typically goes way beyond your own personal benefit. God's command for you to obey him often includes his plan to bless others through you. For example, Tony's obedience has produced significant blessing in the lives of some homeless people in Austin.

Before you stall in your obedience to God, think about who else stands to gain by your obedience. You will probably quickly realize that the impact of your obedience, or disobedience, goes way beyond you.

In early September of 2005, thousands of Hurricane Katrina victims made their way to Austin. Some of the first arrivals were housed in a local school district's athletic facility. These dear people were in significant shock, had lost everything, and in many cases didn't know if all their loved ones had survived the storm. They languished for days at the facility until housing could be found for them.

On the first day that some of the survivors came to Austin, I felt a gentle leading of the Spirit to drive down to the facility, try to meet a few of the survivors, and just take them to lunch. I thought that I could offer a few of them a brief distraction from their chaos. When I got to the facility, I told the security guard what I wanted to do. He disappeared inside and came out a few minutes later with three haggard-looking folks—a young man, his girlfriend, and her twelve-year-old cousin. They had lived through a terrifying and exhausting few days. Over lunch, I heard their stories and learned that there were about thirty more people in their group. When I dropped them off back at the facility, I promised to try to help them.

What happened next still astounds me. As people in my church heard about this group's needs, the offers for help came pouring in. Within just a few days, we were able to

63

find apartments for all thirty people in their group and a few others as well. We completely furnished their apartments and helped them secure free rent for six months, which FEMA was offering. It was the largest outpouring of money, materials, and volunteer effort in our church's history. Several of the families attended our church until they moved back to New Orleans. One family decided to stay in Austin and plant a church. We helped them get started.

The impact of that weekend is still being felt in our church today, years later. Our involvement with those Katrina survivors helped push our missions ministry to the forefront of our church. It helped us see the impact for good that we could have if we were willing to give and sacrifice generously. It also showed many in our church the great joy that comes with serving those who can't return the favor. At the time of this writing, our church gives at least 20 percent of our annual revenue to missions. We are praying and planning to do more. We still send large groups of men, women, and children each year to the Gulf Coast to help with the ongoing Katrina restoration effort. We also send them to places such as Managua, Nicaragua; Juarez, Mexico; and Guatemala.

We can trace the momentum of the missions movement in our church to Labor Day weekend 2005, when we decided to help a few Katrina survivors. And we can trace that to my seemingly small decision to obey a leading to take a few people to lunch.

Set Your Faith Free

God will use your obedience. He'll use it to change you and bless others. Pray for an instant ORT. You don't want to miss the adventure God has for you or hinder the blessing

64

he has for others. Pray Mark 1:17–18 for yourself: *Lord, when you call me, please give me the courage to instantly obey you. Help me to drop whatever I'm doing and follow you.*

6

Did I Just Say That?

Prayers for a Guarded Mouth

Set a guard over my mouth, O LORD; keep watch
over the door of my lips.

Psalm 141:3

Recently my family and I made the short drive from our home in Austin to Waco, about a hundred miles north. You know Waco—home of the Texas Ranger Museum, the original Dr Pepper factory, the Brazos River, and, of course, Baylor University, my alma mater. It was homecoming, and I was looking forward to seeing some old friends.

My buddy Steve Carrell and I used to travel together and lead revival meetings. Steve is now music director at First Baptist Church of San Antonio. Our paths don't cross nearly enough. So, when I heard that Steve was in Waco for homecoming, I immediately started looking for him. My search didn't take long. As I rounded the corner near the Baylor "Bear Pit" (yes, it's where they keep the "bears"), I saw my friend Steve. He had that same goofy grin and looked like he'd lost a few pounds. He was talking to three rather large college-age young men and didn't see me.

Now, if you're a guy, you run into a friend you haven't seen in years, and you want to pick up right where things left off, what do you do? You harass him. You insult him. You tell him how bad he looks, and so on. If you were suddenly nice to him, he wouldn't feel loved, and he would wonder what was wrong. So, in classic "Man, it's great to see you; you look terrible" form, I yelled at Steve from about ten feet away: "Hey, why don't you just shut up?" Steve stopped his conversation with the three giant man-boys, turned, and stared at me, recognition not yet showing on his face. Knowing it would be only a moment before my good friend recognized me and saw the humor in what I was doing, I said it again, only a bit louder: "That's right, why don't you just shut up?"

What happened then was all kind of in slow motion. As the three giants simultaneously turned and snarled at me, I came to the troubling realization that the man I was being so rude to *wasn't* Steve. He looked like Steve, sounded like Steve, and acted like Steve, but he wasn't Steve. And I had just yelled at him to shut up—twice.

Open Wide and Say Nothing

I think the biblical writer of Ecclesiastes showed great wisdom when he exhorted his readers to be men and women of few words (see Eccles. 5:2). For me, the more I speak, the greater the opportunity I have to say something that will hurt someone. James, the half brother of Jesus and the writer of the New Testament epistle that bears his name, also knew the deadly power of the tongue. He wrote:

> Likewise the tongue is a small part of the body, but it makes great boasts. Consider what a great forest is set on fire by a small spark. The tongue also is a fire, a world of evil among the parts of the body. It corrupts the whole person, sets the whole course of his life on fire, and is itself set on fire by hell.
>
> All kinds of animals, birds, reptiles and creatures of the sea are being tamed and have been tamed by man, but no man can tame the tongue. It is a restless evil, full of deadly poison.
>
> With the tongue we praise our Lord and Father, and with it we curse men, who have been made in God's likeness. Out of the same mouth come praise and cursing. My brothers, this should not be.
>
> James 3:5–10

I stand guilty as charged. I've used my words to hurt those I love, to exaggerate, to lie, to overpromise, to curse, and to insult. James said it well: "This should not be!" Like toothpaste once it's out of the tube, harmful words are impossible to recall once you've said them.

So pray for your tongue. The biblical writers have given us ample ammunition for pinpoint praying so that our words will honor God and not hurt others. Here are a few verses you can use as pinpoint promises when praying for your words:

- "He who guards his mouth and his tongue keeps himself from calamity" (Prov. 21:23). Pray that you'll consciously guard your words. When you're out with friends and the conversation turns into a gossip session or the group becomes critical of another person, pray for the strength not to participate. When you're in an argument with your spouse, friend, or roommate and the verbal darts start flying, pray for the wisdom and strength not to say something that you'll regret later. When you're in a job interview or making a sales pitch, pray for the self-control not to overstate your abilities or make claims about your product or service that aren't true. Pray that you'll think about your words before you say them.

- "Set a guard over my mouth, O LORD; keep watch over the door of my lips" (Ps. 141:3). Much like the Secret Service that guards the American president, the king's royal guard would have been an ever-present protective force around David. We don't know what prompted David to pray for a guard over his mouth. Had he just snapped at a palace servant? Had he ridiculed one of his children? Had he made a rash judgment that had cost the freedom or even the life of one of his citizens? We don't know. What we do know is that David found in his royal guard a perfect metaphor for what he wanted God to do with his words. He prayed, *O God, guard my tongue. Place a watch over it. Let no word escape my mouth that would be harmful or dishonorable.* Pray the same. Ask God to protect you and others from the power of your tongue.

- "Simply let your 'Yes' be 'Yes,' and your 'No,' 'No'; anything beyond this comes from the evil one" (Matt. 5:37). I pray this verse for my verbal integrity. It's a vivid statement of how we're supposed to communicate in ways that are clear, honest, and without innuendo. Jesus made this statement when he was teaching against the frequent use of oaths by some of the religious leaders of his day. Instead of swearing by this or that, we simply need to tell the truth. For Christ-followers, *yes* does not mean "maybe," "hopefully," "possibly," or "probably"; it means *yes.* And when we say *no,* it needs to be equally clear of ambiguity or hidden meaning. That's verbal integrity, and we should pray for it. Pray Colossians 3:9 for your words: *Lord, keep me from lying to anyone, since I have taken off my old self with its practices.*

• "Do not let any unwholesome talk come out of your mouths, but only what is helpful for building others up according to their needs, that it may benefit those who listen" (Eph. 4:29). This is a great verse to pray for your words. It doesn't just tell us what not to say, it also teaches us what to say. Here are three specific pinpoint prayers based on this verse.

1. Pray to end verbal corruption. The word *unwholesome* in Ephesians 4:29 comes from a root word that means "corrupt." Corrupt words are the kind that poison and harm others. They don't help; they harm. Pray that no harmful and poisonous words will ever leave your mouth.

2. Pray for verbal edification. Paul commands us to speak words that help and encourage others. Paul's word for *building up* is a construction term. It pictures a house being built piece by piece. Pray that your words will bring strength, security, and growth to the person with whom you're speaking. Even if you need to have difficult or corrective conversations, pray that your words will build up, not tear down.

3. Pray for grace-filled words. When Paul taught that our words should benefit others, he meant that our words should offer grace to the listener. He doesn't mean eloquence of speech but rather eloquence of meaning. Your messages should be kind, truthful, hope producing, and overflowing with grace. Again, even difficult conversations can be grace based. Pray

that your words will give life and hope to the hearer. Pray that your words will always reflect the grace and favor of God.

Set Your Faith Free

Hopefully I've learned my lesson. I plan never to yell "Shut up!" to anyone again, stranger or friend. I'm praying for a pure heart. Jesus taught that our words indicate what's really in our hearts (see Matt. 12:34). If my heart is pure, then my words will reflect it.

Pray the same for yourself. Pray that your heart will resemble the heart of Christ, and that your words will be like his. Pray Psalm 19:14 for yourself: *Lord, may the words of my mouth and the meditation of my heart be pleasing to you.*

7

More Blessed

Prayers for a Generous Spirit

In everything I did, I showed you that by this kind of hard work we must help the weak, remembering the words the Lord Jesus himself said: "It is more blessed to give than to receive."

Acts 20:35

There is a beautiful example of passionate giving found in the New Testament. Mary, the younger sister of Martha and Lazarus, enjoyed a close relationship with Jesus. She, along with her sister and brother, had become safe people for Jesus. They knew him more than just casually. They were close friends. Mary certainly had multiple opportunities to privately express her love for Christ. But the time came when

Mary's private worship of Jesus was no longer enough. She sensed a deep longing welling up inside of her to increase her love and worship of Jesus—even if it meant being misunderstood and criticized.

Mary's inner desire was finally expressed in one of the most powerful and poignant acts of worship and extravagant giving recorded in the Bible. John, an eyewitness to the event, recorded what happened:

> Six days before the Passover, Jesus arrived at Bethany, where Lazarus lived, whom Jesus had raised from the dead. Here a dinner was given in Jesus' honor. Martha served, while Lazarus was among those reclining at the table with him. Then Mary took about a pint of pure nard, an expensive perfume; she poured it on Jesus' feet and wiped his feet with her hair. And the house was filled with the fragrance of the perfume.
>
> But one of his disciples, Judas Iscariot, who was later to betray him, objected, "Why wasn't this perfume sold and the money given to the poor? It was worth a year's wages." He did not say this because he cared about the poor but because he was a thief; as keeper of the money bag, he used to help himself to what was put into it.
>
> "Leave her alone," Jesus replied. "It was intended that she should save this perfume for the day of my burial. You will always have the poor among you, but you will not always have me."
>
> John 12:1–8

What is often lost in the details of that story is the personal sacrifice Mary made when she emptied her perfume jar out on Jesus's feet. Such a valuable commodity could have been sold off little by little and would have provided significant extra income for Mary and her family. Reason and pragmatism suggest that Mary could have demonstrated her love for

Christ just as easily by only using some of the perfume and saving the rest for more practical purposes. But that was not in Mary's heart. She had been gripped by a desire to offer all that she had to Christ. Saving for herself was no longer the point. She wanted to give as generously, passionately, and extravagantly as she could.

A Funny Thing Happened on the Way to the Church

The self-abandonment and giving spirit that Mary showed has, tragically, been lost on this generation of Christ-followers. We have forgotten what Jesus taught us—that when we give to the poor and needy, we give to him (see Matt. 25:40). So even though our gifts and sacrificing may actually benefit a church or ministry, we're still pouring out our love on Jesus's feet. Giving still exalts and honors our Savior. It's unfortunate that he's not getting too much honor these days.

A recent study by the Barna research group indicated that only about 5 percent of Americans actually tithe their income (give away 10 percent or more). Of Americans who claimed to be born-again Christians, only 9 percent gave away 10 percent or more of their income.[1] Stated more bluntly, over 90 percent of Christians in America don't tithe. As a result, ministries and churches face ongoing difficulties because of financial shortfalls. Many Christians simply aren't sharing their financial resources. Few worship Jesus through giving; few are pouring out their love into his body.

The news about church giving isn't much better. A recent study of the nation's largest denominations indicated that only 2 percent of money given to US denominational churches actually gets used for missions.[2] So church lead-

74

ers, who set church policy and are supposed to pave the way and be an example for other Christians, don't seem to have much of a passion for sharing either. It seems the spirit of Mary's extravagant giving is in real trouble in the United States today.

That's actually a bit ironic, isn't it? America isn't just one of the richest countries in the world; it's one of the richest countries in history.[3] The typical American—and that includes an American Christian—lives at a level of comfort and provision unheard of around the world. Our sense of "normal" isn't normal at all. We are a blessed people, but tragically, we're squandering what God has given us.

That's why we need to pray for a heart like Mary's. We need to ask God to make us a people who look for chances to anoint and honor Jesus through our giving to others. We need God to resurrect in us the same spirit that caused him to give his Son for us. Extravagant giving is at the heart of biblical Christianity. We need to pray for God to make us extravagant givers.

Great Reasons to Seek a Giving Heart

Giving is clearly one of the most misunderstood and undervalued disciplines in the Christian faith. Preachers have become notorious for their unrelenting calls for more and more money. The mismanagement by many church leaders of their people's resources has given more than a few Christ-followers a bad taste in their mouths when it comes to giving. That's a terrible shame, because giving is one of the most liberating, joy-producing, and high-impact disciplines in which a Christian can engage. As you pray for a giving spirit like Mary's, here are some things that should motivate you.

Giving Fends Off the Relentless Pull of Materialism

We live in a culture whose mantra is "More is better." More stuff, more toys, more goods, more money, more comfort—the more you have, the better off you are. Unfortunately, many of us have believed that lie. The allure of "more" is quite powerful and attractive. Our nation is filled with countless Christians and churches who have somehow been duped into believing that having nicer things—more comfortable homes and bigger and better church buildings—is what really matters.

Hopefully, you know that it is impossible to satisfy the needs of your God-given soul by throwing stuff at it. Your soul is a spiritual, eternal entity. It cannot be satisfied by anything material. You and I need a life-giving relationship with God through his Son, Jesus Christ. Therein lies our hope for true joy and peace.

Generous giving launches an all-out assault on materialism's death grip on your soul. It helps you push back against the cultural mantra of "more" and reminds you that your hope lies in Christ, not in your stuff. Giving is your way of declaring that the things you own will not own you. It's your declaration of independence from the oxymoron of financial security, and your declaration of dependence on the creating, life-giving God.

Giving Is Good for You

Scientists have been trying to prove for years that having more money does, in fact, make a person happier. Researchers at the University of British Columbia, however, recently found that giving money away actually increases a person's feeling of happiness. Lead researcher Elizabeth Dunn, an assistant professor of psychology, was surprised at how even small adjustments in a person's spending habits can significantly impact his or her feelings. As people altered their budgets to include higher levels of financial philanthropy, their feelings of personal satisfaction and joy increased accordingly.[4]

Once again, science has confirmed something the Bible has been teaching for two thousand years. In Acts 20:35, Luke quotes Jesus as saying, "It is more blessed to give than to receive." A thousand years earlier, King Solomon taught the same thing when he wrote, "A generous man will prosper; he who refreshes others will himself be refreshed" (Prov. 11:25). Christians who are disciplined givers know that these verses teach an important spiritual principle: if you want to benefit your soul, expand your heart, and increase your joy, then give generously.

Giving Blesses Others

Perhaps the personal benefit we gain from giving comes from the others-centered nature of the act. Giving is one of the most selfless acts we can engage in, and it's one of the most rewarding. I believe it's rewarding *because* it's selfless. There is something invigorating about being involved in a work with the sole purpose of helping others.

A group of adults in our church just returned from a seven-day mission trip to Guatemala. They spent their time working in an orphanage, painting fences, doing minor repairs, and holding babies. They served and poured themselves out for seven days, completely for the benefit of others. You would expect that they would return home weary and emotionally exhausted from the trip. But that wasn't the case. They came back glowing! Their week of service had done more to energize their souls than any vacation or personal perk ever could. That's the principle that Jesus taught: it really is more blessed to give than to receive.

I learned this lesson firsthand several years ago when I took a sabbatical from my job. I was graciously given eight weeks off from my work at church. I spent the first six weeks in my favorite playground—the Colorado Rockies—climbing fourteen-thousand-foot peaks with my son. I spent the seventh week in Reynosa, Mexico, working with our youth group to build three houses for impoverished families. I wasn't prepared for what I learned and felt: after six weeks of my dream vacation in Colorado and one week of very hard work in one-hundred-plus-degree heat in Mexico, I felt more fulfilled and enriched by the week of hard labor. The fact that I was sweating, working, and exhausting myself completely for the benefit of someone else—with no visible payoff or payback for me—was one of the greatest and most rewarding experiences of my life. I've been back every summer since.

You want a giving heart because your gifts of time, love, and money will richly bless and give hope to someone else. You'll become a conduit of God's grace and encouragement to someone who desperately needs them. You'll also know levels of joy and personal exhilaration that you can't experience outside of giving.

God Honors Giving

One of the most vivid promises in the Bible regarding giving is found in the Old Testament book of Malachi. You may be familiar with it: " 'Bring the whole tithe into the storehouse, that there may be food in my house. Test me in this,' says the LORD Almighty, 'and see if I will not throw open the floodgates of heaven and pour out so much blessing that you will not have room enough for it' " (Mal. 3:10).

It is difficult to overstate the significance of God's promise to those who faithfully give. In the context of Malachi, God promises to pour out uncontainable blessings on those who fulfill the Old Testament commands regarding tithing. And there is a principle in that verse and many others regarding God's response to giving. Simply stated, he honors giving.

I'm not here to sell you on giving as some kind of kingdom get-rich-quick scheme or tell you that you'll live in luxury if you tithe. Neither idea is biblical. What is biblical is that it is impossible to outgive God. If you give, God promises to give back to you "a good measure, pressed down, shaken together and running over" (Luke 6:38). Any consistent giver will swear to the reality of that promise. Give, and God will give back to you—sometimes financially, sometimes through relational favor, sometimes with increased intimacy with him, and sometimes with a general anointing on your life.

Susie and I both grew up in homes that taught tithing. As a result, we've given a minimum of 10 percent of our income to churches and ministries every month of our marriage. We've seen firsthand the favor and blessing that come through our financial stewardship. We would never stop giving. It's been too much fun and far too rewarding to see how God blesses our obedience.

Pray for a giving and generous heart. Pray for the discipline to give your best gifts to God's kingdom work. Once you start giving, you'll never go back.

The Power of Generosity

On April 16, 2007, the day of the tragic shootings on the Virginia Tech University campus, I was standing on the exposed foundation of a building in Chalmette, Louisiana. I was there with two elders from our church and a local pastor. The foundation was all that was left of his church's building. It had been completely destroyed by Hurricane Katrina.

The pastor, Derek Buchert, was making a valiant effort to reclaim all that the storm had taken. His hometown of Chalmette had been completely devastated. In the year after Katrina hit, most of the churches had decided to relocate in other, less flood-prone areas. As a result, there was no spiritual voice in the town. The residents were left to face their despair and devastation with no church support. In the year after the storm, the suicide rate in Chalmette was the highest in the country.

Derek and his wife, Bonnie, refused to leave. They knew that God had called them to the area and that they had to stay. They chose to suffer the hardships of rebuilding with the people who also remained behind after the storm. But they had no place to meet. The little prayer chapel on their campus that the storm had spared was too small to house their church. They needed a new space—but they couldn't afford anything.

While we were standing on the foundation talking and praying, Derek pointed to an empty auto repair shop across the street. It would be the perfect location for Derek's church to move into while their building was being rebuilt, but the owner wanted far more in rent and finish-out costs than the church could afford. That's when the spirit of extravagant giving—the kind shown by Mary when she poured her costly perfume on Jesus's feet—kicked in. One of the two elders from our church immediately got on his cell phone and started making calls. Within the hour, he had approval from our missions team to officially adopt Derek's church as one of our sponsor ministries, and he had commitments from the members of his small group to fund the lease on the repair shop—three thousand dollars a month—for an entire year.

Within a few weeks Derek was able to move his congregation into his new and fully furnished facility. They also began offering the only functioning children's ministry in the area. Today the church is growing, lives are being given hope and spiritual encouragement, and families are being discipled. The ultimate impact of that one elder and his small group's generosity will be impossible to measure.

That's how giving works. It spreads, grows, and multiplies. It gives hope and encouragement. And it changes lives.

Set Your Faith Free

Are you willing to pray the spiritually revolutionary prayer of asking for a giving heart? I don't believe that generosity just happens. Unless you have the spiritual gift of giving, becoming an extravagant giver like Mary might be a struggle for you. It isn't always natural to look for ways to let go of your resources. Conventional wisdom teaches that we should hang on to what we have, not release it.

I'm just greedy and selfish enough to be tempted by the allure of more. That's why I pray for a generous spirit. That's why I'm asking God to teach me to give. I want to be a giver, but I know I won't become truly generous if I don't invite the Holy Spirit to change me.

Pray for a generous, giving spirit. Pray for a heart like Mary's that looks for opportunities to give extravagantly to the Lord Jesus. Pray that you will sow generously and give cheerfully, and that God will equip you to be a blessing to others (see

2 Cor. 9:6–8). Pray 2 Corinthians 9:12–13 for yourself: *Lord, I pray that as I give, those who are blessed by my giving will overflow with thanks to you. I pray that your people will be led to praise and bless your name because of the gifts you've allowed me to offer.*

8

In Jesus's Name

Prayers for Spiritual Authority

You, dear children, are from God and have overcome them, because the one who is in you is
greater than the one who is in the world.

1 John 4:4

Janie wasn't quite sure what was going on. Whatever it
was, she knew she didn't like it. She also knew that she
needed help. It had started as a simple, vague feeling—kind
of a heaviness. Janie even had felt a little sad at times, but she
didn't know why. She remembers feeling tired, and she had
very little energy for important things.

The vague, heavy feeling lasted several days. As it lingered,
Janie's emotional condition deteriorated. Her close friends and
family told her that she was uncharacteristically irritable and
prickly. She was having more conflict over seemingly insig-

nificant things, and she didn't possess the energy or desire to walk through the appropriate relational mending processes.

Janie was beginning to think that maybe she was sick or depressed. Then things got crazy. In the span of three days, her husband lost his job, her teenage daughter wrecked her car, their refrigerator quit running and had to be replaced, and they had two random overdraft charges from their bank. After all that, Janie no longer thought she was sick; she thought she was losing her mind!

As Janie was telling a close Christian friend about her feelings and the string of "bad luck" that her family had been through, she made a connection she hadn't seen before. About three weeks earlier, Janie had decided to start praying more faithfully for two unbelieving friends. She knew that they were both at pivotal places spiritually and that they needed serious prayer. Janie had covenanted with God to pray and fast for them. And that was when her trouble had started. Her vague and heavy feelings had begun almost immediately after she had started praying more for her friends.

The Christian friend Janie was talking to smiled at her, then said, "Janie, I know what's going on. This isn't bad luck. You're not depressed, and you're not going crazy. You're being oppressed, and we're going to pray right now in Jesus's name that Satan will leave you alone."

A Biblical Reality

While *oppression* is not a biblical term—at least not in the sense in which it's used most frequently today—it is a very biblical concept. When we as Christians speak of spiritual oppression, we're talking about the persistent increase of satanic resistance or an all-out satanic attack on a believer's life. Oppression can be as subtle as the vague heaviness that Janie felt or as overt as the attacks on Job's family and livelihood recorded in the second chapter of Job. But oppression is real, and it is most commonly seen in the lives of Christians who are serious about living for Christ and building his kingdom.

The Bible gives us much insight into the reality of oppression. Biblical writers in both the Old and the New Testaments believed and talked about the work of Satan and his demonic hordes in the world. But it was the apostle Paul who offered the most detailed instructions regarding oppression:

- In 2 Corinthians 2:10–11, Paul called for forgiveness within the church so that "Satan might not outwit us." He then commented that "we are not unaware of his schemes." The implication is that the devil is indeed planning ways to damage and create chaos in Christ's church, and we should be neither naive nor ignorant concerning his works.

- In 2 Corinthians 11:14, Paul taught that Satan was crafty enough to masquerade as "an angel of light" and thus greatly deceive believers.

- In 2 Corinthians 12:7, Paul admitted to having a "messenger of Satan" tormenting him. In this case, God actually allowed the demon to continue its work as a means of keeping Paul humble and dependent on God.

- In Ephesians 4:26–27, Paul warned believers about prolonging their anger and thus giving the devil a place, or foothold, in their lives.

- In Ephesians 6:16, Paul instructed Christians to "take up the shield of faith, with which you can extinguish all the flaming arrows of the evil one."

- In 1 Thessalonians 2:18, the apostle shared with the Thessalonicans that he had tried to visit them on previous occasions but Satan had thwarted his plans.

- In 1 Timothy 5:14–15, Paul warned Timothy about the real temptation young widows faced of being lured away from Christ into a life of following Satan.

From these verses and others like them, we can discern several realities about the devil. Consider just these few:

- He is extremely powerful and well organized.
- He is totally opposed to God and anyone who loves and serves God.
- He works around the clock to thwart and hinder the ministry of the Holy Spirit in and through believers in the world.
- He is capable of deceiving and even leading astray followers of Christ.
- Big biceps, rock-hard abs, or a loaded bank account are totally useless when it comes to opposing Satan.

If you are a Christ-follower, you need to know that Satan is your number one enemy. He will do anything to make you as ineffective as possible in your walk with God, and he doesn't play fair. The biblical writers taught these truths not to scare us but to prepare us. If you're going to live the spiritually fruitful and joyful life that God calls you to, then you have to know how to fight back against the devil. And prayer for yourself is going to be your primary weapon.

We Win

When Jesus died on the cross and rose from the dead three days later, he totally and completely broke Satan's back. The two primary weapons the devil had at his disposal—sin and death—were overcome by Christ in his victorious triumph that we celebrate on Easter weekend. Jesus's death and resurrection gave notice to the powers of darkness that their days were numbered.

In Colossians 2:15, Paul taught that after Jesus "disarmed the powers and authorities, he made a public spectacle of them, triumphing over them by the cross." Paul's readers knew all about public spectacles. They had seen more than a few defeated kings made sport of publicly before being led off to execution. They most certainly understood the weight of Paul's teaching: Satan has been beaten; his doom is sure.

As you pray about your plan to fight back, you need to do so from the standpoint of a victor. You do not stand against the devil as a lone soldier or as one who is part of a battle with an uncertain outcome. You resist Satan as a soldier who is part of an army that has already won the war. There may still be battles and skirmishes to be fought, but the outcome is not in question. Moreover, you fight these battles not just as a soldier but as a prized son or daughter of the conquering king. All the power of your Father's kingdom is available to help you in your battles against your archenemy.

Get on Your Knees and Fight like a Christian!

For me, the hardest part of a long hike or climb is the trip down from a mountain summit. I'm tired from the hike up, and with every jarring step my knees and feet remind me of the many miles and hours I have traveled. Beyond that, mountain summits have clear, cool, and fresh air, breathtaking vistas, and very little noise. But as you descend into the valley, the summit conditions give way to heat, traffic noise, and crowds of people. For me, there is always a bit of a letdown when I come back to "reality" after a long hike.

Jesus, no doubt, felt the same letdown after his trip to a mountain summit with Peter, James, and John. During their time on the mountain, Jesus had actually taken on some of his original, eternal glory. His disciples had the unique privilege of seeing Jesus in his most natural, divine state. Then Moses and Elijah appeared and began talking with Jesus. A voice from heaven spoke, affirming Jesus as God's Son and commanding the disciples to listen to him.

We don't know how long this glorious transformation lasted for Jesus, but it must have been incredibly powerful for him. For a brief time he was able to shed the terrible confines of human frailty and reembrace his divine, eternal nature. He was able to gain encouragement and perspective from two kingdom warriors and hear his Father once again affirm his holy Sonship. There was just one problem with this experience for Jesus: it had to end. He had to come down from the mountain, resume his leadership of a bumbling band of disciples, and face his date with a cross for sins that weren't his.

As soon as Jesus, Peter, James, and John came down the mountain, they discovered that the other disciples were in a heated discussion with a man whose son was possessed by a demon. The demon had made the boy both mute and extremely violent. He was a threat to himself and to others around him. The man brought his son to Jesus's disciples in hopes that they would drive out the demon and save his boy's life, but his disciples had been unable to help the boy. Even after the disciples' best efforts, the demon remained in full control of his young victim.

After rebuking his disciples for their lack of faith, Jesus commanded the demon to leave the child. The evil spirit threw the boy into a brief seizure and then left. The child was whole. When the crowds had left and Jesus was once again alone with his disciples, they asked him why they were unsuccessful in driving out the demon. Jesus answered with one of the most profound and important lessons ever given about the nature of resisting the work of Satan. He said, "This kind can come out only by prayer" (Mark 9:29).

In the realm of rebuking and overcoming the power of the devil, prayer is your most important weapon. Why? Because prayer takes the battle out of your hands and places it in God's. Prayer is the means by which you call on the power of heaven to defend you from the wiles of the devil. It's also how you gain the discernment to recognize Satan's schemes and the wisdom to know how to oppose them. If you're serious about winning your battles against the devil, then you'd better get very comfortable with prayer.

All Authority

Because Jesus is more powerful than Satan, and ultimately because of his victory at the cross, Jesus has full authority over Satan. I don't claim to know how all this works in the spiritual realm, but I do know that Satan and his demons have to do what Jesus tells them to. I know that the devil only has the operating capacity that God allows him. I also know that, because I'm a Christian, I have Jesus's authority in me.

Whenever Jesus sent out disciples in his name, he would deputize them with his authority. Mark tells us that Jesus called the twelve disciples and then "sent them out two by two and gave them authority over evil spirits" (Mark 6:7). Luke writes that Jesus called the Twelve together and "gave them power and authority to drive out all demons and to cure diseases" (Luke 9:1). Jesus knew that as his followers went out proclaiming his kingdom, they would inevitably run into demonic resistance. Part of his commissioning process included giving them the spiritual authority they needed to rebuke the powers of darkness.

At Pentecost, when the Holy Spirit became a permanent part of believers' lives, the spiritual authority of Jesus also became permanent. The deputizing process became final. As Christians, we have power over Satan by nature of our being born again. We are joint heirs with Christ and thereby share in his spiritual power (see Rom. 8:11, 17).

Because of that, we don't have to sit quietly by and suffer the kind of demonic abuse that Janie experienced—we can fight back. Jesus has given us the spiritual authority to oppose and overcome Satan. If we don't use that authority, it's our fault and it's to our own spiritual detriment.

Pinpoint Prayers for Overcoming the Devil

So how do we oppose Satan? If prayer is the key to spiritual victory, then what do we pray? We've already seen that there is a close connection between pinpoint praying and the Scriptures. I believe that the most effective prayers a believer can pray are those that are solidly based in the language and thought of God's Word. And the principle of praying scripturally is never more important than when fighting Satan.

Jesus modeled how important the Scriptures are in spiritual warfare in his own temptation encounter with the devil. As the deceiver tempted Jesus after his long fast in the wilderness, Jesus answered by quoting from the Old Testament. Jesus's threefold "it is written" declarations rebuked Satan, exposed his lies, and established Jesus's position of authority over him. By quoting God's Word, Jesus reminded the devil that he wasn't in the battle alone but had the full power of God and his Word behind him (see Matt. 4:1–11).

When you, a friend, or a loved one are being oppressed and need to pray against demonic forces, here are three powerful scriptural prayers you can use.

Satan, in Jesus's name, you are defeated, because the God who is in me is greater than you are. (See 1 John 4:4.) The overcoming power that you have as a believer has nothing to do with your own abilities or spiritual strength. It's based entirely on Jesus's victory over Satan on the cross. But based on your status in Christ, you are indeed able to claim victory over the devil and his works. The Holy Spirit who lives in you is more powerful than the evil spirit that opposes you. Thus, when you are in a season of spiritual oppression, remind Satan, in Jesus's name, that he is defeated. Remind him of your place of authority over him because of God's Holy Spirit within you. Remind him of your victory in Christ. You are holy ground, and Satan can't change that. Don't put up with his lies and abuse.

Satan, in Jesus's name, I resist and oppose you. Leave me now! (See James 4:7.) I learned the power of this prayer when I was in high school. Whenever I would feel depressed or face temptation, I would speak out loud against Satan. I would tell him that, in Jesus's name, he had to leave me. What typically happened next made a huge impression on me as a young Christ-follower. Feelings of peace and love would flow over me. My feelings of fear or temptation would almost immediately subside. I learned that because of my authority as a Christ-follower, I could command Satan to leave me, and he had to obey.

I've used the promise of James 4:7 on countless occasions in my life, and I'm quite sure I haven't used it enough. I don't have to sit quietly by while Satan tempts me, harasses me, and tries to lead me astray—and neither do you. Pray the powerful pinpoint prayer that Jesus made possible for you through his death. Learn to resist Satan in Jesus's name. He will leave you.

Lord, please show me the areas of my life I may have unwittingly yielded to Satan. Help me to identify and rid my life of these strongholds through your grace and power. I pray that you will help me make every thought I have subject to Jesus Christ. (See 2 Cor. 10:3–5.) Satanic strongholds are areas where Satan knows he can push your buttons. They're areas of weakness in which you are more susceptible to falling prey to the devil's schemes and lies. For one Christian it's a struggle with fear; for another it's self-image. One believer may struggle with a stronghold of greed; another may wrestle with bitterness and unforgiveness. Many Christians today have strongholds of lust; many others battle significant levels of insecurity. Whatever the issue, spiritual strongholds are areas in which Satan has unusual pull and influence over a Christian.

While I may be bold, courageous, and strong in many areas, I can still have a stronghold in an area of my life in which my ability or even my desire to resist Satan is almost nonexistent. And my strongholds are most often mental. That's why the apostle Paul instructed us to make every *thought* captive to Christ. We are not to give any room for thoughts of fear, worry, hate, prejudice, lust, or greed to be cultivated in our minds. We must, by God's grace, discipline our minds to rebuke any stray thought that might give Satan a foothold to start tempting us and lying to us. As a Christian, you don't have to be subject to the strongholds of sin that devastate so many believers. Pray for God to help you make every thought captive to Jesus. Pray with Paul that your mind would dwell on whatever is true, noble, right, pure, lovely, admirable, excellent, or praiseworthy (see Phil. 4:8).

Set Your Faith Free

Don't wait until the trouble hits to start praying about the authority you have. Bathe your life—your thoughts, attitudes, and actions—in prayer every day. Pray for Jesus's protection over them. Pray for the discernment to recognize Satan's schemes. And when you pray against your spiritual adversary, pray out loud. I don't know why this is so important—I'm sure it has something to do with the way things work in the spiritual realm—but it is critical in the battle against the devil. When you pray against him, tell him verbally and in Jesus's name that he is defeated. Don't just think your prayers against Satan, say them out loud. Doing so will have a dramatic effect on the spiritual climate around you.

A member of our staff wrote to me recently about the importance of praying out loud against the devil:

> I pray out loud, especially when we are under attack—you know, the times when the nightmares are terrifyingly real and fear runs rampant in the middle of the night. It is during those times that the most effective prayer for us is to claim God's truths out loud before we go to sleep and pray for him to post swift and mighty angels around our bed to do battle for us while we sleep. I can't count how many times I've woken my husband in the middle of the night, proclaiming not-so-quietly that I am a child of the Lord Jesus Christ. Leave me alone, Satan. You know I am spoken for.

Don't be Satan's punching bag. Don't put up with his spiritual terrorism. Fight back! Jesus died to give you authority over the devil. Use it! Don't ever forget that you are holy ground. Don't let Satan forget it either.

Pray this pinpoint prayer for yourself: *Lord Jesus, thank you for the authority over Satan that you gave me through your death. Thank you that I have overcome him by your blood.*

Thank you that as I resist him, he must leave me. Please give me the mental discipline to bring every thought under your holy authority. Please make me brave and proactive when it comes to praying your protection over my life, over my friends and loved ones, and over my home. Help me to embrace the power you have given me as your child and to become effective at resisting the devil's work in my life. I pray this in the holy name of Jesus. (See 1 John 4:4; Rev. 12:11; James 4:7; 2 Cor. 10:5; and Eph. 6:10–18).

9

How to Move a Mountain

Prayers for Your Faith

The apostles said to the Lord, "Increase our faith!"

Luke 17:5

It may be one of the most memorable moments in Hollywood history. It's certainly one of mine. Indiana Jones—complete with jacket, distressed leather hat, and trusty bullwhip—stands on the ledge of what appears to be a bottomless crevice. He is in search of the most prized find of archaeology, the Holy Grail. In order to reach the Grail, Jones has to get across the crevice. But there is no discernable way across. Sheer rock walls line both sides of the deep ravine. There are no vines to swing from, no rickety footbridges to cross, and no ways around. It appears that if Dr. Jones wants to get to the Grail, then he is going to have to step out into thin air.

The Grail's journal, compiled by Jones's father, calls this crossing a "leap of faith." The drawing in the journal shows a brave knight walking successfully over the gorge, seemingly on nothing but air. Jones closes his eyes and takes a deep breath. After a few moments, he slowly raises one leg straight out in front of him. It's an awkward stance—he almost resembles a wooden toy soldier in a marching position. Then Jones lets his weight fall forward. He is past the point of no return. If anything is there—any invisible means of support—Jones's extended leg will land right on it. If nothing is there, Jones will begin a cartwheeling fall that might just last for eternity.

You probably know what happens next. Jones is indeed caught by a previously invisible stone ledge that extends all the way across the ravine. It only became visible when he left the security of the ledge and stepped out in faith.

Is that how faith really works? Is it a blind leap in the dark? Does faith require us to leave our realms of security and safety and step out into the unknown with little or no evidence that there is anything there to catch us? Or is faith clearer than that? Is it more calculated, more certain, and less like a free fall? How important is faith in a Christ-follower's life, and how do we develop it?

Living by Faith

Prayer is the currency of God's kingdom. It's how things get done in the rule and reign of God. Faith has a different but equally vital role. In the kingdom of God, faith is like air. We simply can't live without it.

Everything having to do with God requires faith. The entire process of thinking about him, seeking him, obeying him, worshiping him, and serving him involves faith. God is an intangible, infinite being. Because of that, we have to learn to relate to him in the realms of belief and hope.

That's why Jesus and several New Testament writers placed such an emphasis on belief. They understood the relationship between faith and functioning in God's kingdom. Here are just a few of their comments:

> When Jesus heard this, he was astonished and said to those following him, "I tell you the truth, I have not found anyone in Israel with such great faith."
>
> Matthew 8:10

> [Jesus] replied, "You of little faith, why are you so afraid?" Then he got up and rebuked the winds and the waves, and it was completely calm.
>
> Matthew 8:26

> Some men brought to him a paralytic, lying on a mat. When Jesus saw their faith, he said to the paralytic, "Take heart, son; your sins are forgiven."
>
> Matthew 9:2

> For in the gospel a righteousness from God is revealed, a righteousness that is by faith from first to last, just as it is written: "The righteous will live by faith."
>
> Romans 1:17

> We live by faith, not by sight.
>
> 2 Corinthians 5:7

> I have been crucified with Christ and I no longer live, but Christ lives in me. The life I live in the body, I live by faith in the Son of God, who loved me and gave himself for me.
>
> Galatians 2:20

Now faith is being sure of what we hope for and certain of what we do not see.

Hebrews 11:1

As you can see, faith is an integral part of kingdom living. Jesus applauded those who manifested faith, rebuked those without it, and honored those who acted on it. The apostle Paul knew that the only way to live and function in God's kingdom was through faith. For him, every step, breath, and action were part of his faith walk. Paul had developed a new set of eyes, so to speak. He had learned to look at life through the lens of faith in Christ. We need to pray for the same spiritual vision.

Why Faith Matters

Everything—and I do mean *everything*—that we hope to accomplish in our lives as Christ-followers requires faith. Faith is the backdrop against which we live our Christian lives. It's the stage we act on, the field we play on, and the house we live in. It is impossible to segregate faith from Christianity. One requires the other.

Faith is the logical next step after knowledge. Through faith, we take what we understand to be true about God and move in the logical direction that our knowledge and experience dictate. Faith leads us from the arenas of facts to logical conclusions. But it's still faith. When it comes to dealing with God, we can't truly know anything empirically (the realities of God can be neither reproduced nor measured in any material way), so the entire process of relating to God is a faith venture.

That's why we need to pray like the disciples did: "Increase our faith!" (Luke 17:5). Praying for faith is like adding air to a low tire. It will help us move along more effectively and efficiently in God's kingdom. Here are a few biblical reasons to pray for increased faith.

Faith Pleases God

The writer of Hebrews got right to the point when expressing his understanding of faith: without it, you can't please God (see Heb. 11:6). The means by which humans connect with God is faith. Without faith, you'll never be able to have a relationship with him. Faith opens the door to knowing, loving, and serving God.

But the writer of Hebrews wasn't finished. He also said that God rewards you when you have faith, "because anyone who comes to him [God] must believe that he exists and that he rewards those who earnestly seek him" (v. 6). While it's true that faith is required to please God, it's also true that God honors those who believe. God's desire is for all people to seek him. When you choose to do so, when you acknowledge the pull of God in your heart and approach him through faith, he rewards your choice to believe.

According to the writer of Hebrews, God is not like a mean and scary wizard who tries to intimidate and chase off all who would dare to approach him. Rather, God is the kind and approachable Creator of the universe who honors and blesses those who approach him in faith. He wants a relationship with every one of us.

You want to be a person of faith, because it is the means by which you can approach, know, and relate to God. God will honor your desire for faith. Pray that your faith will grow.

Faith Sees What Others Don't

In 2 Kings 6, Elisha and the armies of the king of Israel were surrounded by the armies of Aram. The king of Aram was intent on attacking and killing all the Israelites. When Elisha's servant woke up in the morning and saw that they were surrounded, he immediately panicked. He cried out to Elisha, "Oh, my lord, what shall we do?" (v. 15).

His concern is understandable. From an earthly standpoint, they were in big trouble. In a matter of moments, he and his countrymen could be either captive or dead. But Elisha didn't share his servant's concern. He was either immune to fear or unaware of the immediate danger—or he knew something his servant didn't. Actually, Elisha saw something that his servant hadn't yet seen.

After hearing his servant's cry of concern, Elisha responded, "Don't be afraid. . . . Those who are with us are more than those who are with them." The writer then tells us what happened next: "And Elisha prayed, 'O LORD, open his eyes so he may see.' Then the LORD opened the servant's eyes, and he looked and saw the hills full of horses and chariots of fire all around Elisha" (vv. 16–17).

Faith is the ability, by God's grace, to see what others don't. It's the capacity to look into insurmountable circumstances and find the hope and provision of God, even when those around you can't. Faith is having the awareness of God's kingdom in the world, even when no one else around you knows it's there. Jesus taught that all who are born again can see God's kingdom (John 3:3); it's by faith that you do. Faith opens your eyes to the power of God in your daily life, and it is impossible for you to experience the abundant life that God promised without it.

Faith Opens the Door to the Miraculous

Matthew 13 records what I believe is one of the saddest verses in the Bible. Jesus had spent a frustrating few days in his hometown of Nazareth, and "he did not do many miracles there because of their lack of faith" (v. 58). There is an obvious relationship between faith and God's willingness to work miraculously. The verse doesn't say that Jesus *couldn't* do miracles in Nazareth; it says he *didn't* do miracles there. It seems that God doesn't feel obligated to work where his power is doubted.

Faith is the key that unlocks the treasury of God's unlimited resources. It paves the way for the presence and anointing of God. The relationship between faith and God's power is simple: if one is not there, you won't find the other either.

But the reverse is true as well. God is ready and willing to work in miraculous ways wherever faith resides. Had the people of Nazareth not doubted Christ, the verse could just as easily have read, "Jesus did many miracles there because of their great faith." What a difference faith makes!

If you want your life to be a place where God's power resides, then you want him to find faith residing in you. Pray for great faith. Pray that your belief in the presence and power of God would be a conduit for his supernatural work in and through you.

A Little Faith Goes a Long Way

This is really great news for those of you who struggle with faith. The fact is, you don't have to have large amounts of faith to have significant kingdom impact. Jesus went to great lengths to show his disciples just how accessible mountain-moving faith was to anyone who wanted it. On one occasion, Jesus offered the following metaphor: "I tell you the truth, if you have faith as small as a mustard seed, you can say to this mountain, 'Move from here to there' and it will move. Nothing will be impossible for you" (Matt. 17:20).

The image of the mustard seed was quite common in Jesus's day. The mustard seed was tiny and unimpressive (picture a tiny kernel of birdseed). It would have been difficult for the disciples to think of anything much smaller. So what was the point Jesus was making about faith? He was teaching that a little faith goes a long way. He was trying to teach his disciples—and us—that they had more faith than they realized.

There is something you need to know about faith: if you're a Christian, you already have more than a mustard seed's worth of faith. At some point in your life, you had enough faith to pray and ask God to save you from your sins. You believed that a holy God would grant you forgiveness and favor based on the death of his Son. That was a HUGE act of faith on your part—way more than a mustard seed's worth. And that's a perfect starting point for you to ask for *more* faith.

Too many Christians view themselves as faith weaklings. In reality, you can't become a Christian without faith. So stop believing that you don't have any faith and start praying like you do. Then pray for more. God will give it to you.

Set Your Faith Free

There are a multitude of verses you can use as pinpoint prayer builders for your faith. Here are just a few:

- If you feel a battle raging between your faith and your fears, pray Mark 9:24: *Lord, I do believe! Help me to overcome my fears and unbelief.*
- If you have trouble believing what you can't see, pray John 20:29: *Lord, you affirmed those who had faith in you without seeing you. Please help me to believe even though I don't fully see.*

102

- If you struggle with having the hope that faith produces, pray Romans 15:13: *God of hope, I ask you to fill me with all joy and peace as I trust you, so that I may overflow with hope by the power of the Holy Spirit.*

Faith isn't reserved for great theologians or monks who lock themselves away in a monastery. Faith is an everyday fruit that can and should be yours on great levels. Pray for a profound faith. Pray that your faith will please God. Pray that your faith will fuel your kingdom walk. Pray that you might be like Stephen, an early church leader. Pray Acts 6:5 for yourself: *Lord, give me a heart like Stephen's. Please make me a person of faith and full of the Holy Spirit.*

10

Get Out of the Boat

Prayers for Your Courage

Be on your guard; stand firm in the faith; be men
of courage; be strong.

1 Corinthians 16:13

It was, no doubt, a highly unusual command. The soldiers
were used to taking orders, but typically their orders made
some sense. Not today. On this day, the order seemed crazy.
It was a complete waste of time. Maybe the searing heat and
lack of water had finally gone to their commander's head.

What was the order? Dig ditches and trenches—as many
as possible, because a flood was coming. Why was it crazy?
Because they were in the middle of the desert!

The king of Judah had joined forces with the kings of Israel
and Edom to fight against the king of Moab. After a difficult,

seven-day march through the Desert of Edom, a rugged area located southeast of the Dead Sea, they ran out of water. The soldiers and horses were weak and tired. If the armies of Moab found them in their weakened state, they would be sitting ducks. The kings summoned Elisha the prophet and asked him for guidance from the Lord. Elisha responded, "This is what the LORD says: Make this valley full of ditches. For this is what the LORD says: You will see neither wind nor rain, yet this valley will be filled with water, and you, your cattle and your other animals will drink. This is an easy thing in the eyes of the LORD; he will also hand Moab over to you" (2 Kings 3:16–18).

The kings gave the order, and their men went to work digging ditches in the desert. It must have been quite a sight. What happened? Scripture tells us, "The next morning, about the time for offering the sacrifice, there it was—water flowing from the direction of Edom! And the land was filled with water" (v. 20).

Faith and Courage

It took faith to believe that God would send water in the desert, but it took courage to start digging ditches. Courage is the first cousin to faith. Where faith believes, courage acts. Where faith trusts, courage moves. Where faith looks up, courage steps out. Courage is the God-given ability to act on what you believe. As a good friend of mine says, "Courage puts feet to your faith."

Consider the example of Peter and the rest of the disciples. After a long day of ministry, Jesus ordered his disciples to cross the Sea of Galilee without him. Later, in the middle of the night, Jesus came to them by walking across the water. Peter, in his classic speak-first-and-think-later style, asked Jesus if he could join him on the water. That's faith. Peter believed that Jesus could sustain him if he stepped out of the boat.

But believing that Christ can do something and giving him the opportunity to do it are two different things. It took faith for Peter to believe that Jesus could support him, but it took courage for him to get out of the boat. That's the difference between faith and courage: the former believes; the latter acts.

So what happened to Peter? Why did he start sinking? Matthew, an eyewitness to the event, tells us, "But when he saw the wind, he was afraid and, beginning to sink, cried out, 'Lord, save me!'" (Matt. 14:30). At first Peter lost his courage. He started looking around at the waves and the sea, and he lost his nerve. Then he lost faith. As Jesus rescued him, he rebuked him for his failed beliefs: "Immediately Jesus reached out his hand and caught him. 'You of little faith,' he said, 'why did you doubt?'" (v. 31).

Faith and courage are so closely related that the level of one will no doubt affect the other. As your faith increases, courage to act on it will frequently follow. But if your courage wanes, you might also begin to lose your faith. That's why we need to pray for both—for the faith to believe God and the courage to act on it.

Lord, Please Send Courage, and Hurry!

Several years ago, the Lord led me to take our church to a new level of obedience and faith. It concerned the often sticky subject of church finances—particularly, how we budget for our ministries. I became convicted that the way we planned our budgets required neither the miraculous work of God nor much faith from us.

You probably know that in most businesses and churches, budgets are set on the basis of projected revenues. Typically their budget number will be less than or equal to what they think they'll receive in sales (for businesses) or gifts (for churches). I began to feel that God wanted us as a church to try something different, something a little more radical. It's what we now call vision-based budgeting, and the inspiration for it comes from Matthew 14.

Jesus had been addressing a very large crowd of men, women, and children. The number of men alone was five thousand, so you can imagine just how large the crowd was. When it started to get dark, the disciples urged Jesus to send the crowds away so they could get home safely and still have time to find food for themselves. Jesus responded with a simple statement that must have sent chills down the spines of his disciples: "They do not need to go away. You give them something to eat" (Matt. 14:16). With those few words, Jesus gave the disciples an assignment that was totally impossible for them. They simply didn't have the resources on hand to feed such a massive group. But Christ wasn't thinking about *their* resources; he was thinking about *his*. He wanted the disciples to see that their abilities as kingdom leaders weren't going to be based on the best they could do; they would be based on the best God could do.

Therein lies the scriptural principle for vision-based budgeting. We began asking our staff what they believed God was calling them to do in their respective areas of ministry. Then we would come together as leaders and pray about the overall ministry year and budget we would need. Inevitably, the God-given vision and budget for the year would far exceed our projected receipts. That's when we had a choice to make. Do we play it safe and budget on what we think we'll get, or do we follow God's vision and budget for what only he can do?

You probably know what happened in the rest of Matthew 14. Jesus told the people to sit down, and then he commanded his disciples to organize them into groups of fifty (see Luke 9:14). They were preparing them for a meal from resources that currently didn't exist. That took both faith and courage. It took faith to believe that Jesus could feed the crowd; it took courage to begin to act on their faith and ask the multitude to stay for dinner. Jesus prayed over the little food that they had and then multiplied it miraculously. In the end, they had more food left over than when they had started. (For a full-length version of this amazing story, see Matthew 14:13–21.)

Today, we're several years into the vision-based budgeting process. It has been an incredible adventure, but it has not been easy. Our faith has been tested repeatedly. We've had seasons of huge, unexpected financial surplus, and we've had seasons of belt tightening and nail biting as we waited for God to come through. But he always has. I can honestly say that none of us in leadership would ever go back to our former "safe" system of budgeting.

But this walk of faith has taught me something about myself. I believe that God will come through—I have a high gift of faith anyway, so trusting in God's provision isn't difficult for me—but what I often lack is courage. I believe (sometimes I could even say I *know*) that God will provide for us. But I'm often terrified of moving forward based on my faith. The "what if" scenarios always start to play out in my head. So when people ask me these days how they can pray for me, I typically respond with one word: courage. I need the courage to act on what I believe God is going to do. If you're a typical Christ-follower, I bet you could use some courage too.

The Importance of Courage

The importance of courage in the lives of God's people is clearly evident in the Bible. In the first chapter of Joshua,

God exhorted Israel's new leader to be brave and strong. Joshua, who had grown up at Moses's side and seen all of the great works that God had done, had plenty of faith. What he needed as a leader was the courage to act on it. So God called him to be courageous:

> Be strong and courageous, because you will lead these people to inherit the land I swore to their forefathers to give them.
>
> Joshua 1:6

> Be strong and very courageous. Be careful to obey all the law my servant Moses gave you; do not turn from it to the right or to the left, that you may be successful wherever you go.
>
> verse 7

> Have I not commanded you? Be strong and courageous. Do not be terrified; do not be discouraged, for the LORD your God will be with you wherever you go.
>
> verse 9

> Whoever rebels against your word and does not obey your words, whatever you may command them, will be put to death. Only be strong and courageous!
>
> verse 18

Note that with each of the Lord's exhortations to Joshua to be brave came the command to lead or obey. Courage is required for action.

The disciples of Jesus also modeled the power of courage in the lives of believers. In the months following Jesus's resurrection, the church exploded in growth. Thousands and thousands of people joined the ranks of this fledgling and outlawed movement. Because of that, Jesus's original disciples were given larger and larger platforms for leadership. They also drew the ire of the same group that had opposed and eventually crucified Jesus.

But as we noted in chapter 4, the disciples' proximity to Jesus had a major emboldening effect on them. Again, note the summary statement of Jesus's enemies about his disciples: "When they saw the courage of Peter and John and realized that they were unschooled, ordinary men, they were astonished and they took note that these men had been with Jesus" (Acts 4:13). Peter and John had great faith. They had walked with Jesus, had seen him die, and then had seen him on several occasions after his resurrection. And their faith yielded great courage for them. They stood firmly in the face of severe opposition and even possible arrest because of their brave spirits.

The apostle Paul, arguably the most influential Christian who ever lived, struggled with courage. His letters are filled with references to his own battles with fear. Who can blame him? What human, having been repeatedly stoned, beaten, whipped, shipwrecked, and betrayed by his own countrymen, wouldn't have fear issues? But God wasn't going to let fear control the apostle. He repeatedly spoke to Paul and called him to be brave.

When Paul was just beginning his ministry in Corinth, the Lord appeared to him and said, "Do not be afraid; keep on speaking, do not be silent. For I am with you, and no one is going to attack and harm you, because I have many people in this city" (Acts 18:9–10). In Jerusalem, after Paul had almost been killed by an enraged mob, the Lord again spoke to him: "Take courage! As you have testified about me in Jerusalem, so you must also testify in Rome" (Acts 23:11). God's command for Paul to speak in Rome gave him the courage he needed to stand firm and not fear for his life while in Jerusalem.

Later, while on the way to Rome, the ship Paul was sailing on endured a horrible fourteen-day storm. All hope was lost for any rescue. But once again God called Paul to be courageous. He appeared to him and promised that Paul would indeed testify before Caesar in Rome (see Acts 27:23–24). And Paul, while imprisoned in Rome and not sure if he would live or die, wrote to the believers in Philippi, "I eagerly expect and hope that I will in no way be ashamed, but will have sufficient courage so that now as always Christ will be exalted in my body, whether by life or by death" (Phil. 1:20). Even in the face of an uncertain future, Paul showed great courage.

Paul was a man of tremendous faith. He knew the Lord Jesus personally and powerfully. But his faith didn't always preempt his fear. He needed courage. He needed the spiritual gusto to walk forward with what he believed. That's what courage is, and that's what each of us needs as we seek to live Christ-honoring lives.

Courage in Action

In a recent edition of *Newsweek*, author and radio personality Garrison Keillor was asked to list the five most important books in his life. Surprisingly, Keillor cited the book of Acts as the most important book he had ever read. When describing Acts and the courage of those early Christians, Keillor noted, "The flames lit on their little heads and bravely and dangerously went they onward."[1]

I love those three words, "bravely and dangerously." When the disciples went out in Jesus's name, they presented a great danger to the powers of darkness. Sure, they faced ongoing dangers to themselves, but they were also dangerous to the enemy. I too want to be a dangerous Christian, and moving out in faith-based courage is where dangerous Christianity begins.

Here are a few examples of what Christian courage looks like in everyday life:

- Courage is the couple writing their first tithe check to their church, even though they don't think they have the money, because they feel led to be better stewards of their financial resources.
- Courage is the thirty-year-old woman breaking up with her boyfriend of two years because he is unable to lead her spiritually.
- Courage is the young Christian intern at a law firm who refuses to cut corners on billing procedures, even though it might cost him a promotion.
- Courage is the young pastor preaching against a particular sin in his church, even though he knows that his words will offend many people.
- Courage is new parents taking a major cut in income so that the mother can stay home with the baby, trusting that God will provide what they need.
- Courage is the eighth-grade Christian boy who refuses to experiment with drugs, even though just about every one of his friends is pressuring him to.

Pray for your courage:

- Pray for the courage to honor God, even if it means you lose favor with people.
- Pray for the courage to practice immediate obedience, even if it will cause difficulty for others.
- Pray for the courage to speak God's truth and to share his love with others when given the opportunity.
- Pray for the courage to confess your own sins and to seek the forgiveness of others when necessary.

- Pray for the courage to be authentic in relationships and not to hide your feelings.
- Pray for the courage to stand for what is right and true, even if it means standing alone.
- Pray for the courage to go where God leads you, to do what God tells you, and to become what God is calling you to be, even if it is way beyond your comfort zone.

Set Your Faith Free

Pray for your courage. Pray that, like Joshua, you will be strong and courageous. Pray that, like Paul, you will be given the courage to overcome your personal fears. Pray that, like the early disciples, you will move out bravely and dangerously into Satan's territory. And pray that, like Jesus, you will have the courage to walk the path that God sets before you. Pray 1 Corinthians 16:13 for yourself: *Father, equip me to be on my guard and to stand firm in the faith. Make me a person of courage, and make me strong.*

11

I Must Become Less

Prayers for the Gift of Irrelevance

He must become greater; I must become less.

John 3:30

When my accountability partner, Rick, and I pray for each other, we have an unusual request. We pray for the gift of irrelevance. As I pray for myself, I've started using the word *invisible* a lot. Perhaps I should explain.

I am the leader of a large, rapidly growing, and relatively well-known church in my city. Because of that, I have somewhat of a platform. I run into people who attend our church just about every time I go out. My friend Rick leads a counseling ministry that specializes in affair recovery. His ministry is affecting lives all over the nation. He has become a high-profile leader.

Rick and I both know that the larger the platforms we have, the larger Satan's bull's-eye is on each of us. We also know that we are very likely to fall prey to the sin of pride and the sense of entitlement that goes with it. That's scary to both of us. And since neither of us has any desire to become a kingdom-harming headline because of our sin and arrogance, we've started praying that we won't matter. We pray for irrelevance. We pray that we won't want fame or any type of popularity. We pray that we would crave invisibility and be very content to stay below the radar of the Who's Who in God's kingdom.

Less Is More

Praying for invisibility is a very biblical concept. John the Baptist is the biblical character I think of first when it comes to having the proper perspective of his place before the Lord. In the months preceding Jesus's baptism, John's ministry was soaring. He was the first prophetic voice to be heard on Israel's religious landscape in four hundred years. And as John's popularity increased, so did the talk about his being the Messiah, bringing deliverance from Rome, and returning the people to the glory days of Israel. Had John had an ego and any desire to misrepresent himself as the savior of Israel, he certainly could have. But John repeatedly pointed people away from himself and told them to look to Jesus instead.

One day, John's disciples confronted him about his apparent lack of ambition. They sensed that Jesus's ministry was bypassing John's, and they could tell that they were about to end up on the wrong end of the pendulum swing of cultural popularity. When they asked John why he seemed so content to play second fiddle to Jesus, he answered:

No one can receive anything unless God gives it from heaven. You yourselves know how plainly I told you, "I am not the Messiah. I am only here to prepare the way for him." It is the bridegroom who marries the bride, and the best man is simply glad to stand with him and hear his vows. Therefore, I am filled with joy at his success. He must become greater and greater, and I must become less and less.

John 3:27–30 NLT

John's response goes down as one of the clearest explanations of the "it's not about me" mind-set ever recorded in history. His words make great fodder for pinpoint praying about your place and role in God's kingdom.

In the face of my own ego and my fleshly desire to be "somebody," I've learned to pray John's words for my life: *Lord, you must increase; I must decrease.* Pray that for yourself as well.

Kingdom Bragging Rights

If there was ever a believer who could have argued for his spiritual supremacy and his rightful place as a Christian celebrity, it was the apostle Paul. Paul's dramatic conversion was the stuff of legends, and God's use of him was unmatched by any other human at that time. And yet Paul shunned the spotlight. He refused to be recognized as a hero or a mover and shaker in God's kingdom.

In his first letter to the Christians in Corinth, Paul rebuked the church for arguing over what Christian leader should be the most popular and should have the most influence in the church (see 1 Cor. 1:10–17). He wanted no part of a Christian popularity contest. Paul, like John, had plenty of opportunity to tout his résumé and to assert himself as the chief of

Christians. Instead, he claimed to be the chief of sinners (see 1 Tim. 1:15). Paul made it very clear to the Corinthian believers that they were to put their hope in Christ, not in him. Listen to his self-effacing words:

> When I came to you, brothers, I did not come with eloquence or superior wisdom as I proclaimed to you the testimony about God. For I resolved to know nothing while I was with you except Jesus Christ and him crucified. I came to you in weakness and fear, and with much trembling. My message and my preaching were not with wise and persuasive words, but with a demonstration of the Spirit's power.
>
> 1 Corinthians 2:1–4

If a guy like Paul didn't seek kingdom fame, then neither can we. Pray 1 Corinthians 2:2 for yourself: *Lord, I pray that the message of my life would be Jesus Christ and him crucified.*

Brother Wallisch

There are no "celebrities" in God's kingdom. There is no room for powerful people or big egos. Jesus taught that if you want to be first, you have to be last. The kingdom has only one star, one hero, one leader. All the rest of us are just followers. Any fleshly desires I have to be a bigwig in God's kingdom are completely unbiblical. If I truly want to be great, then I have to become invisible.

The Lord made this point very clear to me several years ago. On May 11, 2000, I was enjoying a one-day silent retreat with several other pastors at a Catholic retreat center outside of Chicago. During the morning hours, I walked the pristine grounds, quietly meditating and enjoying the Lord's presence. I was on my way back to my room when a massive thunderstorm rolled over the conference center. Several inches of rain fell on us over the next few hours.

When the rain first started to fall, I stayed outside under an overhang, taking in the sights, sounds, and smells of the storm. It was beautiful. That's when I noticed the garden. About fifty yards away under some gorgeous trees was a lovely prayer garden. At one end was a huge cross. It stood majestically, keeping watch over the rest of the garden. A footpath led up to it, and on either side of the path were stone markers in the ground. They looked like small tombstones, but they didn't seem far enough apart to be graves.

I stood in my dry place for a few minutes, just looking at the rain-soaked garden scene before me. The more I looked at it, the more compelled I felt to look closer. This may seem strange, but I felt moved to look at the garden right then, while it was raining. I didn't feel like I was supposed to come back later and have a nice walk through the lovely garden when it was dry and warm. I felt this strong pull to leave my place of safety right then and to explore this garden in the rain. And I was pretty sure God was leading me to do it.

So I stepped out. I walked slowly toward the garden and then turned and stood at the head of the footpath facing the cross. I was immediately drenched, so I no longer felt the need to hurry. (After a while, wet is wet.) I paused for a moment, then began walking toward the cross.

The stones on either side of the footpath were indeed grave markers. There were dozens of them, each with a name. They appeared to be the burial spots of Catholic priests who had served in the area over the last century.

I stopped in front of the stone right next to the cross. It read, *Bro. Lawrence Wallisch. B. June 8, 1885. D. June 1, 1941.* What struck me was that I had never heard of Brother Wallisch or any of the men who were buried there. These weren't people who'd written great books or been war heroes or famous movie stars. They weren't politicians or even famous clergymen. They were just servants—faithful servants.

By this point the rain was coming down harder. It seemed to increase in intensity with every step I took toward the cross. So I turned and faced the cross and asked the obvious question: *God, why do you have me out here? What is it you're trying to tell me?*

And then I got it. God clearly spoke to me as I was out there in the rain, surrounded by gravestones at the foot of the cross. What he said went something like this: *Will, are you willing to be obscure? Are you willing to live your life for me and go unnoticed? Do you require stardom and fame to remain faithful to me? Do you expect it as payback for following me? Are you ready to live your life fully for me, to die, and then, fifty years later, to have no one remember or care that you'd even lived? Are you willing to be unimportant? Will, there's room in Christianity for only one superstar, and that place is reserved for the one who died on the cross. All the rest of you just get to be servants.*

I've been praying for the gift of irrelevance ever since May 11, 2000, when I took my place next to Brother Wallisch on the path up to the cross. I learned something eternally significant that day: in our faith, there is room for only one star. The only appropriate place for a Christ-follower is at the foot of the cross, both in life and in death.

In his classic devotional, *My Utmost for His Highest*, Oswald Chambers writes:

> It is one thing to go on the lonely way with dignified heroism, but quite another thing if the line mapped out for you by God means being a door-mat under other people's feet. Suppose God wants to teach you to say, "I know how to be abased"—are you ready to be offered up like that? Are you

ready to be not so much as a drop in a bucket—to be so hopelessly insignificant that you are never thought of again in connection with the life you served? Are you willing to spend and be spent; not seeking to be ministered unto, but to minister? Some saints cannot do menial work and remain saints because it is beneath their dignity.[1]

Set Your Faith Free

Pray for the gift of irrelevance. Pray for freedom from the desire to "be somebody" in God's kingdom. Pray for the willingness to accept your assignment from God and to serve him fully and passionately, regardless of the visibility or perceived importance of the task. Ask God to make you content to take your place at the foot of the cross, alongside all of his other followers. Pray Galatians 6:14 for yourself: *Lord, may I never boast except in the cross of our Lord Jesus Christ.*

Part 3

Fuel for the Fire

Practices That Enhance Your Prayers for Yourself

While they were worshiping the Lord and fasting, the Holy Spirit said . . .

Acts 13:2

Great praying never happens in a vacuum. The kind of praying that gets things done in God's kingdom is never accidental or random. Neither is it the work of an unyielded life. Great praying is fueled by a submitted, disciplined life.

Prayers that change you are the same. Pinpoint prayers for yourself are most effective when coupled with the timeless disciplines that add fuel to the fire of your praying. In this part, I want to show you how to increase the passion, the anointing, and the impact of your personal prayers. I want to help you learn to mingle high-impact spiritual practices with your pinpoint praying so that your prayers bear much fruit and yield true kingdom results in your life.

If you apply the practices discussed in the following pages with the principles of pinpoint praying that you've already learned, then you will be changed. You will be an open, pliable vessel in God's hands. You will get out of your spiritual rut. You will have more joy. And you will become more of the holy follower of Christ that God wants you to be.

12

Learning the Bible

Jesus answered, "It is written: 'Man does not live on bread alone, but on every word that comes from the mouth of God.'"

Matthew 4:4

I recently spent a week in Reynosa, Mexico, with about thirty ninth graders from our church. We went there to build two small houses for two impoverished families. This was my third such mission trip, and I enjoy it more each time. I'm also learning some important lessons about home building.

When we first arrive at the work site, we're anxious to get started. We have four days to complete the house, and we don't want to let our family down by not finishing the job. The temptation is always to start building walls and making roof trusses without doing a good job on the house's foundation and flooring. I've learned the hard way that if we don't build a good foundation—if it's not level or square—then the rest of the house's structure will be compromised. A half inch of poorly laid foundation can translate into several inches of misaligned walls and roofing, which means the house will be unstable, and the roof will leak and won't last very long for the family we're trying to serve.

So, we don't rush when laying the foundation. Even if doing so takes most of the first day, we make sure we get the foundation right. It's just not worth it to have to go back and correct it later.

Many of us as Christians face a similar temptation when it comes to our approach to the Bible. Busy schedules and to-do lists tempt us to skimp in our Bible reading. As a result, many of us have developed a drive-by mind-set when it comes to God's Word. We blow through our devotionals, not giving them the time and attention we should to really benefit from them. In other words, we build a poor foundation for our daily lives.

In Matthew 7:24–27, Jesus talked about the importance of making his Word the foundation for our lives. He said that if we're going to survive the storms of life, then we need the firm foundation that only God's Word can give.

When it comes to reading the Bible, the point is not to see how quickly we can get through it. Rather, the point is to see how much of the Bible we can get through us. When it comes to understanding the profound messages of God's Word, there are no shortcuts. And, when it comes to being equipped to pray powerful pinpoint prayers for your life at a moment's notice, you want as much of the Bible in you as possible.

Take a Little Faith, Mix In Scripture, and Then Pray!

We've already seen just how important the Scriptures are in pinpoint prayers. Remember? Pinpoint prayers are specific and biblical. I've already shown you how to use your Bible as your prayer script. But what do you do when you don't have your Bible with you? How do you pray true pinpoint prayers if you don't have access to God's Word? There's only one way: you learn it.

The Bible is the most potent, potentially explosive document in the world. More than mere literature, the Bible is the living Word of God. That's why you want it hidden in your heart and mind. You want to be ready to draw from its wisdom when you need it.

Consider these awesome claims the Bible makes about God's Word:

- It never withers or fades away, and it abides forever (Isa. 40:8).
- It accomplishes God's purposes (Isa. 55:11).
- It is the sword of the Spirit (Eph. 6:17).
- It trains you in righteousness (2 Tim. 3:16).
- It is living, active, and sharper than any two-edged sword (Heb. 4:12).

With all this going for it (and many more qualities I didn't list), the Bible is without exception the best tool to have in your hands when you're pinpoint praying. But when you can't have it in your hands, you want it in your head and heart.

How to Get the Bible in You

The great news about learning the Bible is that it's never too late to start. There is a former Jew in our church who came to

125

Christ in his early sixties. At the time, he knew very little about the Bible. But his hunger to know Christ led him to become a true student of God's Word. In just a few short years he became very much like another Jewish convert to Christianity—Apollos, whom Luke described as "mighty in the Scriptures" (Acts 18:24 NASB). So, regardless of your age or your current knowledge of the Bible, you can still become well acquainted with the message and meaning of the Bible. If you're not already, start taking the steps today to get God's Word in you. Here's how.

Read It

We talked earlier about the importance of a daily quiet time when mining the Bible for pinpoint promises. But I want to mention it again briefly here. When it comes to learning God's Word, there is no substitute for the simple exercise of regular Bible reading. And the good news is that, like so many other areas of a relationship with God, a little bit of effort goes a long way.

Every time you spend a few minutes or a few hours in the Bible, you give God more scriptural content to work with when leading you to pray pinpoint prayers for yourself or others. Each session of Bible reading only increases the amount of Scripture you have stored up in your heart. Those verses become a rich reservoir of knowledge that you can tap whenever you feel prompted to pray the Word, even if you don't have a Bible nearby.

It doesn't matter if you haven't been reading the Bible for many years. What does matter is that you get started. God will honor the effort. The discipline of Bible reading is very much like tithing. Even if you don't think you can afford to, go ahead and do it anyway. God will honor it and will reward you for the time you invest in his Word.

Study It

A fellow pastor at our church, Gary Sinclair, has an interesting method of studying the Bible. He picks out fifty-two chapters in the Bible that he wants to learn more about, and then he focuses on one chapter a week for a year. This gives Gary the opportunity to contemplate the meaning of each chapter he studies and to become very familiar with its teachings. During each week, he'll read a few different translations, study different commentaries, make personal notes, and, most importantly, read the chapter over and over. By the time the week ends and it's time for Gary to move on to another chapter, he is very familiar with the one he's been studying.

That's how you get God's Word in you—study it. Give it more than just a cursory glance. Gary's method may not be the one you use, but find a method that works for you and start using it. The Bible is the greatest book ever written. It's worth your while to study it, and it will make you more effective in your pinpoint praying.

Meditate on It

Meditating on a certain verse or verses of the Bible is one of the best ways to get the Word in you. Bible meditation is unlike the meditation taught in Eastern disciplines. Eastern meditation encourages you to clear your mind of all thought and seek a mental interaction with an abstract idea or concept. There's nothing abstract about biblical meditation.

When you meditate on a verse of Scripture, you're trying to saturate your brain with its message and meaning. You want to align every thought you have with the powerful truth of the verse you're praying over. If you can learn the simple practice of Bible meditation, you'll find your mind filled with ever-increasing amounts of God's Word.

One method of meditation I use involves saying the verse out loud over and over. Each time I say the verse, I emphasize a different word. For instance, suppose I'm praying over and meditating on 1 John 1:9: "If we confess our sins, he is faithful and just and will forgive us our sins and purify us from all unrighteousness." I might read or say the verse one time through completely, then start over. I would emphasize the first word (*if* we confess our sins . . .), then the second (if *we* confess our sins . . .), then the third (if we *confess* our sins . . .), and so on. I follow that pattern until I've gone through the entire verse.

As you can see, every time you emphasize a different word, further meaning comes to light. By the time you've emphasized each word in the verse, you've begun to capture the true essence of what the verse is saying. And then you're well on your way to having that verse stored forever in your memory.

This method of Bible meditation makes you slow down and deal with the substance of the verse. There will be times when you may want to read several chapters in a day. There will be other times, however, when you will want to saturate your brain with a particular biblical promise. Meditation helps you do that, and it will also make you a much more effective pinpoint pray-er.

Memorize It

Perhaps the most effective way to add Scripture to your head and heart is to memorize it. Scripture memorization may involve a little more effort, but it's well worth it.

I have the privilege of praying with individuals and groups of believers just about every day of the week. I can tell when

I am praying with someone who knows the Bible. Inevitably, he or she ends up praying the Scriptures. People who have memorized parts of God's Word are some of the most powerful pinpoint intercessors I know. The Bible just flows out of them. I always feel inspired, encouraged, and even a little cleaner after I've prayed with someone who knows much of God's Word. Praying the Bible out loud and from memory just seems to attract the sweetness of God's presence.

Now, don't be intimidated by this. Even if you don't know any verses from memory, you can quickly learn one or two and start using them in your prayers. Let me help you here. If you don't know it already, why don't you memorize John 14:14: "You may ask me for anything in my name, and I will do it." We talked earlier about what it means to pray in Jesus's name. It means that you believe you are asking for something that Jesus himself would pray for. You believe it's completely consistent with God's will. So learn John 14:14 and start reminding God of it in your prayers. Say, "Father, you said that if I ask in the name of Jesus, agreeing with his purpose and plan, then you would give me what I pray for. Well, Father, I believe that this is the very thing that Jesus would pray for. I believe that this is completely consistent with his heart and passion. And because of that, I ask you now to give me what I ask for."

Do you see how adding just one verse of Scripture to your prayer gives so much power and authority to it? Think of the boldness and authority with which you could approach God if you knew dozens or even hundreds of verses. So why wait? Start memorizing God's Word, and then start adding it to your prayers. You'll be amazed at the difference it will make in your praying.

Memorizing verses of the Bible doesn't have to be hard and painful, but it does require some effort. Here are just a few suggestions for committing Scriptures to memory:

- *Use flash cards.* Write your verses on small index cards, and keep the cards with you. Go over them at red lights; say them while on a coffee break or lunch break at work; practice them before you go to sleep at night; recite them while you're doing chores.

- *Write them out.* Pick two or three verses you want to learn each week, then write them out every day. Before the week is over, you'll be able to write them from memory.

- *Sing them.* Music has an incredible way of sealing words in our minds. I'm amazed when I can still sing every word of a song I haven't heard in years. So sing your Scriptures. Make up little tunes or use tunes you already know. Singing verses of the Bible will help you learn them in no time.

- *Learn them with a friend.* A friend of mine trained for a marathon with a friend of his. They decided to learn a verse of Scripture for every mile of the race—that's twenty-six verses. Every mile they had a new verse to focus and meditate on during their grueling run. You can do the same. Get your accountability partner or a member of your small group to learn the same verses you are. You can take turns reciting the verses to each other on the phone or writing them by memory and emailing them to each other. The camaraderie and even the competition of having a partner in your memorizing efforts will make it much easier and more motivating for you to learn.

Pinpoint Promises When You Need Them Most

A few years ago, my wife was involved in a terrible car accident. She was traveling on a curvy road west of Austin on a rainy day. A large delivery van that was traveling too fast lost control and swerved across four lanes of traffic, hitting Susie's car head-on. We credit God and excellent Volvo safety engineering for saving Susie's life. She walked away from the accident with only a few scrapes and bruises. The car was totaled.

In the moments before the accident, Susie had been praying and meditating on some verses from Deuteronomy 28. In that great chapter, the Lord promises to make Israel "the head, not the tail" and says that the nation would "always be at the top, never at the bottom" (v. 13). It's a beautiful promise about obedience: God will honor his people when they obey him. Susie was thinking about those very words when her reality was suddenly shattered by screaming brakes, breaking glass, a violent impact, exploding air bags, and then confusion and fear.

Several witnesses stopped to offer help to Susie. As they helped her out of the car and guided her to the side of the road where she could wait for the ambulance, Susie remembered the words from Deuteronomy: *You will be the head, not the tail. You will always be at the top, never at the bottom.* Susie immediately started crying and praying those verses over and over. She was overwhelmed by the goodness and grace of God, even in the midst of a terrible and frightening ordeal.

Set Your Faith Free

My wife was able to pray specific pinpoint promises in her time of need because she had them stored up in her heart. You never know when you may need to pray for yourself or others without any notice or without the luxury of having a Bible to guide you. If you want to be fully equipped to pray powerful pinpoint prayers, to be ready in season and out of season, then hide God's Word in your heart. Pray Acts 18:24 for yourself: *Lord, I pray that you will make me mighty in the Scriptures.*

13

Spiritual Breathing

Pray continually.
1 Thessalonians 5:17

Not too long ago, my wife and I got into an argument. It wasn't too big of a deal; I can't even remember what we were arguing about. But it was significant enough to require a cup of McDonald's coffee to fix it. So, somewhere in our conversation I called time-out and told Susie we were going to McDonald's for coffee. She quickly agreed.

On the way to McDonald's, the argument got a little more heated. Susie and I just couldn't seem to find a place of agreement on this topic. As we stood in front of the counter at McDonald's, ready to place our orders, Susie wasn't a happy camper. She was polite to the young lady who was taking our order, but I could tell that she was still put out with me. After Susie ordered her coffee, I did the same. I told the young woman that I wanted a large decaf. Then the girl behind the counter asked a question that I thought I'd never hear. Her six words totally rocked my world—six words that put a new perspective on my tiff with Susie, six words that changed my life forever.

"Do you want the senior discount?"

As she spoke, the words just seemed to echo all around me. Time just stood still for one brief instant. I was dumbfounded.

"Do you want the senior discount?"

She actually asked me again. Now, you need to understand something. At the time of this writing, I am forty-six years old. I don't have any gray hair, and I am in relatively good shape. I am a long way from needing a senior anything. I don't even have senior moments yet. Why would I want a senior discount?

Well, when the young woman asked me her six-word question the second time, Susie burst out laughing. She laughed so hard I thought she might pass out from lack of oxygen. The young woman behind the counter looked terribly confused, as if she had no idea why I was frowning and why my young "daughter" was laughing so hard. Not wanting to solicit any more comments from the discernment-challenged girl behind the counter, and not wanting to give Susie any more entertainment, I paid the girl and slunk off to the nearest booth. And yes, I took the discount.

Six Words That Will Change Your Life Forever

Another six-word statement packs even more punch. It's given to every Christ-follower and can radically transform not just how you pray but how you live. Here it is: "Instead, be filled with the Spirit" (Eph. 5:18). With these six simple words, the apostle Paul invites you into an ongoing, profound relationship with God's Holy Spirit. As you learn to constantly seek the Spirit's filling, you will discover levels of joy and anointing that you hadn't known previously, and you will find it much easier to pray.

In 1 Thessalonians 5:17, Paul exhorted the believers in Thessalonica to "pray without ceasing" (NASB). He called them to a life of unending, unbroken prayer. I don't know about you, but I find it difficult to do just about anything without ceasing. Even the things I love to do—things like eating, hiking, skiing, and sleeping—have their cutoff points. In fact, the only thing I actually do without ceasing is breathe.

Actually, breathing may be exactly what Paul was talking about. I believe Paul was telling us that prayer should be as natural and effortless for us as breathing. We shouldn't have to think about it. Prayers should flow out of us as seamlessly and fluidly as when we inhale and exhale. And when you pray with that much ease and consistency, you'll find that you are more often filled with God's Holy Spirit.

How to Practice Spiritual Breathing

I learned the discipline known as spiritual breathing years ago from some staff members of Campus Crusade for Christ. The phrase was made popular by Crusade founder Bill Bright. Spiritual breathing is one of the most important disciplines I've ever learned. It can have an immediate, positive impact on your life and your prayers.

As you know, breathing involves the nonstop functions of exhaling and inhaling. At least twelve times a minute your body discards the poisonous carbon dioxide left over from the fresh oxygen your lungs took in and processed only moments before. Then, as soon as the toxins are out of your body, you once again draw in a fresh supply of

135

life-giving oxygen. The bad air is replaced with good, and the entire process repeats itself. On a normal day, your body will naturally complete the exhale/inhale process over seventeen thousand times. If the process is halted for too long, you will die.

Spiritual breathing involves the same two natural functions—exhaling and inhaling—but they're spiritual activities, not physical. And they are as vital to your spiritual life as your regular breathing is to your physical life. Let me tell you about each of the two functions in spiritual breathing.

Exhaling

When you exhale, you're literally blowing the bad air out of your body. You remove the toxins and poisons left over after your lungs process the oxygen you've inhaled. Spiritual exhaling involves the biblical discipline of confession, and it allows you to cast off the sins and spiritual toxins that often pollute your soul. It's bringing your sin before God the moment you become aware of it, and then seeking God's forgiveness, healing, and restoration. Spiritual exhaling is based on the wonderful biblical promise of 1 John 1:9: "If we confess our sins, he is faithful and just and will forgive us our sins and purify us from all unrighteousness."

That great promise in 1 John is written to believers. The forgiveness it speaks of is in reference to fellowship and intimacy with Christ, not salvation. When you become a Christian, all your sins—past, present, and future—are forgiven. You are declared holy by God, and you are given the gift of his Holy Spirit's presence in your life as proof of his acceptance of you. But you still sin, and those sins break down the fellowship that exists between you and God.

Sin builds a wall; it separates. Isaiah 59:2 says, "But your iniquities have separated you from your God; your sins have hidden his face from you, so that he will not hear." When you sin, even though you're a Christian, it creates barriers in your relationship with God. Sin won't steal you from him completely or ever cause you to lose the gift of salvation that he has given you, but it does kill intimacy. Sin is very much like having a fight with a family member: when you're in conflict, you're still related, but the tension has hindered your relational intimacy. Only confession and forgiveness can undo the damage that the conflict wrought.

Sin hinders the flow of God's love, grace, and power through your life. The more you allow it to build up, the more it hurts your relationship with Christ. That's why spiritual breathing calls for you to exhale the sin from your life the moment you're aware of it. You don't want to give sin any time to create strongholds and to choke the love of God out of your life. The instant you become aware of your sin, confess it. Take it to God and seek his forgiveness for it. If you sin—you lust, judge, gossip, lie, worry, get inappropriately angry, and so on—a hundred different times in an hour, then you need to exhale that junk from your life in that same hour. That way, you keep your heart and soul clean before God, and you keep his power and love flowing through your life.

Think about your last twenty-four hours. What sins have you committed? Have you confessed them to God? Have you allowed him to cleanse and forgive you for them? If not, then you have twenty-four hours' worth of spiritual poison built up in your life. Stop right now and confess your sins to God. Be as specific as you can. Ask the Holy Spirit to reveal any sins to you that you may not be aware of. Don't leave any stone unturned.

As you exhale, pray Psalm 139:23–24: *Search me, O God, and know my heart; test me and know my anxious thoughts. See if there is any offensive way in me, and lead me in the way everlasting.* Confess whatever God shows you and immediately seek his forgiveness. Then move on to the second part of spiritual breathing—inhaling.

Inhaling

Inhaling is your body's way of taking in a fresh helping of life-giving oxygen. Spiritual inhaling is your soul's way of taking in the invaluable and life-giving presence of God, and it involves pinpoint praying for a very specific command to become a reality in your life. It takes us back to the six words I mentioned earlier that can change your life forever: "Instead, be filled with the Spirit" (Eph. 5:18). When you inhale spiritually, you ask God right then and there to fill you with his Holy Spirit.

Being filled with God's Spirit is not a onetime event. It is not a permanent act, unlike the baptism of the Spirit (also called the "gift of the Spirit" and "sealing with the Spirit"), which occurs at salvation and needs to happen only once (see Acts 1:5; 2:38; 10:45; and Eph. 1:13–14). The Scriptures tell us that God's Spirit can be grieved and quenched (see Eph. 4:30 and 1 Thess. 5:19, respectively) and that the most common culprit in both is our own sin. Thus, while you can't lose the Spirit's presence in your life, you can definitely deplete his filling in your life. That's why you need to pray repeatedly for the Spirit to fill you.

When you are filled with God's Spirit, you are more likely to manifest the fruit of the Spirit that Paul listed in Galatians 5. You will be more prepared to forgive, more prone to be grateful, more inclined to worship, more willing to serve, and more equipped to pray without ceasing. The Spirit's filling in your life will stifle the fleshly, sinful tendencies that hang around just below the surface of your soul, and it will immerse you in Christ's loving, powerful presence.

Ephesians 5:18 ("Be filled with the Spirit") is actually a command in the original language. Filling is not something that God simply wants for all Christ-followers; it's something he requires. Thus, you can know that when you pray for the Spirit to fill you, he will.

Whenever you confess your sins to God throughout the day (exhaling), immediately follow that with a prayer for God to fill you with his Spirit (inhaling). I like to turn my hands palms up as I ask God to fill me. That is a pinpoint prayer you can know God will answer. He wants to fill you, he longs to fill you, and you need him to fill you. When you ask for the Spirit's filling, expect God to answer. Thank him for filling you. Expect to feel different, to be different.

Calming the Storm

During my sophomore year in college, a fraternity brother of mine, Chuck, died in a tragic car wreck. He was on his way to a sorority dance with his date when they were hit by a drunk driver. My friend was killed instantly. Only an hour or two after the wreck happened, I got the call that Chuck had died. My roommates and I had the grim assignment of making our way around campus and telling many of Chuck's closest friends the terrible news.

One girl, Lisa, took the news especially hard. Right there in the lobby of her dorm, she went into complete hysterics. She threw herself on the ground and began to sob and heave uncontrollably. Soon she was hyperventilating. It was one of the most tragic and painful displays of grief I've ever seen in my life. One of my roommates, Layne—a giant of a man—wrapped his huge arms around Lisa and just held her while she wept. As he did, my other roommates and I started praying out loud for Lisa. We asked God's presence to come into the room. We asked him to be enthroned on that scene right then and there. We prayed for the Holy Spirit to fill Lisa and begged him to replace Lisa's grief with a supernatural peace.

Within just a few minutes, the entire scene in that dorm lobby was transformed. Lisa's wails turned to whimpers, and then her whimpers turned to whispers. Her cries of pain gave way to prayers and praise. Then Lisa grew incredibly quiet. She seemed almost like a human version of the divine calm that came to the Sea of Galilee after Jesus rebuked the storm and commanded the elements to be still. Lisa would grieve for months, but her peace had been restored. The Spirit had done his work.

That's what the Holy Spirit wants to do in your life. If you allow him to fill you, he will turn your chaos into peace. He will repair the damage left behind by sin. He will expel the poison of your selfishness and replace it with his life-giving presence. When you pray for the Holy Spirit's filling, in one miraculous instant you too can receive the great calm that only God's presence can bring.

Set Your Faith Free

Are you ready to start practicing spiritual breathing? You have everything to gain and absolutely nothing to lose by trying. Try this simple exercise.

First, exhale. Confess your sins to God. Sit quietly for a few moments and reflect on areas where you may have failed in the last few hours. As things come to mind, confess them to God: *Lord, I confess my impatience with the person in front of me at the coffee shop this morning. Please forgive me. Father, I know I have a judgmental spirit toward Tommy. Please forgive me. God, I've spent more time worrying about my finances than praying about them. I ask you to forgive me.* Then pause and ask God to reveal any sins you have failed to recognize. If any come to mind, confess them immediately.

When you feel like your soul is free from all its debris, inhale. Turn your hands over and place them palms up. Then say something like, *Lord Jesus, I seek the filling of your Spirit right now. I ask in faith that you chase all the junk out of my soul and replace it with your life-giving Spirit. I know this is your will for me, and I thank you now for hearing and answering my prayer. Sweet Spirit of God, fill me now.*

I have been praying prayers like this one for nearly thirty years. I prayed one today. I can honestly say that I still feel different after I seek the Spirit's filling. Even now, I typically get goose bumps and chills. My whole perspective changes.

God really is faithful to his promises. He is true to his Word. If you seek the Spirit's filling for your life, even if you ask more than a hundred times a day, he'll always grant it.

So quit holding your breath. Start breathing. You'll live differently, love differently, and begin to learn what it means to pray without ceasing. Pray Ezekiel 11:19 for yourself: *Holy Father, please give me an undivided heart and put a new spirit in me. Remove my heart of stone and give me a heart of flesh, just as you promised.*

14

Fasting

When you fast . . .

Matthew 6:16

Thank you for not skipping this chapter.

Several years ago a buddy of mine decided to lock himself in a hotel room for three days to fast and seek God. He confessed to me beforehand that he was worried about two main temptations during his three-day retreat. First, he was concerned about the temptation of food—getting too hungry and somehow cheating by ordering something to eat before the fast was completed. Second, he was worried about the temptation of lust. He knew that at some point in the weekend he would have to fight the pull of the hotel's sexually oriented pay-per-view movies.

My friend actually ended his retreat early and came home on the second day. When I asked him why he stopped his retreat so soon, he told me that he knew he was in trouble after his first night in the hotel room. While he was asleep, he dreamed that a beautiful, naked woman had delivered a piping hot Domino's pizza to his hotel room door.

For many of us, my friend's experience sums up our own weak attempts at fasting—great intentions with little or no real results. Just frustration.

Well, for all of us potential fasters, there's still hope. Not only can you learn to fast, you can actually learn to fast effectively. You can even learn to *love* fasting. And, when you see how fasting blesses your life and increases your ability to pray, you'll be glad you made the effort to learn how.

Jesus's Big Three

The Sermon on the Mount, recorded in Matthew 5–7, is Jesus's definitive treatise on kingdom life. In it he tells disciples of both his day and ours the secrets to effective living as his followers. In Matthew 6, Jesus addressed three disciplines that were very common in his Jewish culture. Those disciplines are giving, prayer, and fasting.

One might be tempted to argue that we should seek to apply only the principles of Jesus's message about these disciplines, given the vast differences between his culture and ours. But when we look closely at the teachings of Jesus's great sermon, it's difficult to find anything that isn't still very relevant, and that includes the teaching on kingdom disciplines. In fact, we'd be hard-pressed to find three more needed disciplines for Christ-followers today than giving, prayer, and fasting. Thus, when Jesus said, "When you give" (Matt. 6:2), "when you pray" (v. 5), and "when you fast" (v. 16), I believe he meant that those disciplines were timeless—that they are as valuable to us today as they were in his culture. In other words, if we want to get the most out of our kingdom living, then we need to regularly give, pray, *and* fast.

The Dynamic Duo

Since we talked about giving in chapter 7, let's talk about fasting and prayer here. If you're looking for a powerful one-two punch that can not only thwart Satan's work but also help you and others, then consider combining the two disciplines of fasting and prayer. The characters in many of the Bible's most dramatic stories knew the importance of mingling fasting and intercession. Consider these examples:

- When King Jehoshaphat wanted to seek God's protection from invading enemy armies, he called on all the people to fast and pray (2 Chron. 20:3).
- Ezra called for fasting and prayer when he led many families from Babylon back to Jerusalem to rebuild the temple. They were traveling with large amounts of gold and silver, and they desperately needed God's protection (Ezra 8:21).
- When Mordecai and the Jewish people heard of the king's plan to annihilate the Jews, there was spontaneous fasting, weeping, and praying by all the people as they sought God's deliverance (Esther 4:3).
- Before Esther approached the king to ask for deliverance for her people, she called for three days of fasting and prayer, that she might find favor before him (Esther 4:16).
- When Daniel came to the realization that Judah's captivity in Babylon would last seventy years, he sought

God's favor for his people with prayer and fasting (Dan. 9:3).

- The disciples were praying, worshiping, and fasting when they felt God's leading to send Paul and Barnabas on their first missionary journey (Acts 13:2–3).
- Paul and Barnabas prayed and fasted when appointing elders in the churches they were starting (Acts 14:23).

Our predecessors in the Christian faith believed strongly in the power of fasting and prayer. The answers to prayer they received and the miraculous nature of their ministries are proof that God blessed their fervent, self-denying pursuit of him.

How Fasting Enhances Prayer

After nearly three decades in Christian ministry, I have personally become convinced that there are just some things that only prayer and fasting can accomplish. Fasting adds weight and authority to prayer. Let's talk about how.

Fasting Humbles You

Humility is a great benefit in prayer. A humble person finds favor with God where a proud or haughty person does not. Psalm 34:18 promises that the Lord is near to the brokenhearted and saves those who are crushed in spirit. James 4:10 promises that if you will humble yourself before God, he will lift you up. Humility and effective praying—specifically, praying for yourself—go hand in hand.

Fasting crushes your pride and independence. The strong, self-reliant attitude you may feel when your stomach is full will be quickly shattered after just a few hours of fasting. Fasting is a great way to gain perspective on yourself. It places you in the proper mind-set before God and helps you to approach him with an unassuming and broken spirit. Such humble praying always gets God's attention.

Fasting Helps You Focus

Fasting increases your mental and spiritual awareness. Your stomach pains tend to sharpen your mind. You become more alert, and you'll find you are able to focus for longer periods of time. On days that I fast, I can read the Bible, pray, and write for much longer periods of time, without mental fatigue, than on those days when I'm not fasting.

Thus, fasting adds focus and energy to prayer. A hungry intercessor will typically pray with more passion and zeal than one with a full stomach. Fasting will help you tune in on your conversation with God and avoid those pesky mental distractions that we all face when trying to pray. If you want and need to add passion and mental clarity to your prayers, pray hungry.

Fasting Shows God That You Mean Business

I like to refer to fasting as "turning up the heat" in prayer. Fasting is your way of telling God that you are deadly serious about the designated topic of prayer. It also helps to elevate the seriousness of the prayer issue in your own heart. When you combine fasting with pinpoint praying, you signal to God and to yourself that you are willing to do whatever it takes to secure his answer on the subject at hand.

Occasionally, I'll spend a day fasting and praying over a topic that is very important to me. I am always amazed at how my fast adds to my sense of urgency and intensity about that subject. Sometimes I don't really appreciate just how urgent or important an issue is in my life until I've fasted over it. I can't count the number of times my fasting has led me to say to God in prayer, "Father, you know I'm fasting about this. You know that I mean business. I'm willing to do whatever it takes to gain your answer, your direction, and your favor in this area."

Are you praying for deliverance from a sin? Are you praying for the power to forgive and release a grudge? Do you need wisdom about an upcoming decision? Add fasting to your prayers. It will tell God—and you—just how important the matter really is in your life.

Fasting Increases Your Spiritual Perception

There's something about being hungry that makes you more spiritually alert. Whereas a full stomach can dull your spiritual senses, hunger heightens them. Fasting is a great way to raise your spiritual antennae and tune in to what God is saying and doing.

Isaiah 30:21 says, "Whether you turn to the right or to the left, your ears will hear a voice behind you, saying, 'This is the way; walk in it.'" That's how I often feel when I'm fasting. I am much more aware of God's presence around me, and I am much more likely to detect and correctly interpret his voice. When my stomach is full, I tend to be pretty sluggish spiritually, if not intellectually and physically. But there is something about hunger that adds an edge to my spiritual perception. I've learned that if I really want to hear from God on a matter, then I need to stop eating for a while.

In 1996, I went through a rough time personally. God was doing some serious housecleaning in my life, and repentance, confession, and healing were high on his agenda for me. During that time, I went on a multiday fast. That was unusual for me, as my fasts are typically of the one-day variety. But during that season, I sensed the need to turn up the heat in my petitions to God and to seek his wisdom about myself. I also felt that God was leading me into an extended fast.

I'm glad he did. Toward the end of my fast, I had a vision. I didn't go into a trance or see the heavens part, but I did get a very clear picture in my brain. I'm sure it was from God. I saw a huge rock formation—hundreds of feet high and equally wide. The rock seemed to represent my life— my psyche, my emotions, my inner person. The rock had two layers: the top layer was labeled "Pride"; the bottom was labeled "Insecurity."

I knew immediately what God was telling me. He was saying there were two foundational strongholds in my life that I had to deal with. The bottom and most entrenched of the two was insecurity. At my core, I am a terribly insecure person. I've battled the need to please people and have gone to disastrous lengths to keep from upsetting others and losing their approval. The surface or foremost evidence of my insecurity was pride. Pride isn't a sign of confidence and strength; it's a sign of weakness and fear. I had tons of both.

In that vision God showed me with painful clarity how I needed to begin praying for myself. He was calling me to address the issues deep within me that made me insecure and afraid of the opinions of others. He also wanted me to repent of my arrogance and overconfidence. That was a powerful message. It changed the way I prayed for myself and led to some immediate healing and breakthroughs in my life.

Today I can still see that "rock" image in my mind, and I often refer back to it when praying or thinking about my own spiritual condition. It has also helped me in coaching and counseling others with their security issues.

Are there personal battles you are fighting that you just can't seem to win? Do you have personal strongholds that you can't seem to overcome? Ask the Lord if you should fast about them. If he says yes, then don't hesitate. The results could be life changing.

How to Get Started

Don't panic. I'm the guy who used to think that fasting was skipping my afternoon Milky Way bar. I've learned to fast. You can too. Here are some simple suggestions to help you work your way toward a fasting routine.

- *Pray about it.* Start praying for a desire to fast. I pray that I will be hungry to fast. God will honor your prayers and will give you the faith and courage you need to start fasting.
- *Read about it.* There are many great biblical passages about fasting. My favorite is Isaiah 58:6–12. When I read those inspired words about the impact and blessing of fasting, it makes me *want* to fast. Read that passage and pray that God will call you to that level of spiritual impact.

  There are also many great books on fasting. Two of my favorites are Bill Bright's *Seven Basic Steps to Successful Fasting and Prayer*[1] and Art Wallis's *God's Chosen Fast*.[2] Both will inspire you and offer helpful steps in how to get started.

- *Get support.* If you decide to start a fast, even if it's a short one, then tell a friend and ask him or her to pray for you. Don't worry, you're not violating Christ's command about fasting in secret. You'll find that you need the prayers, and the accountability will be good for you.

- *Start small.* If you're new to fasting, be content to start small. God will honor the heart behind the fast. Try skipping just one or two meals at first. Use the time you would spend eating to read God's Word and pray. Whenever you feel hungry, thank God for the physical reminder your body is giving you to seek him. Turn your brief, physical discomfort into a passion for prayer and seeking God. As your body becomes more accustomed to going without food, and as you get more comfortable with being hungry, you'll find that you actually welcome the hunger pains. At that point, you'll be ready to try a longer fast.

- *Give yourself some grace.* Don't be legalistic about your fasting. If you don't make your full goal the first time, don't be too hard on yourself. Fasting takes time to learn. God is more interested in the attitude that led you to fast in the first place than the actual number of hours or days you spend in the fast. So give yourself room and time to grow in this discipline.

Set Your Faith Free

Are you ready to turn up the heat on your pinpoint praying? Do you want to show God that you mean business when it comes to your prayers? Do you want to humble yourself before God and increase your spiritual alertness? Then start praying about the discipline of fasting. Pray Isaiah 58:6 for yourself: *Holy Father, please call and equip me to fast so that you might work in and through me to loose the chains of injustice, untie the cords of the yoke, set the oppressed free, and break every stronghold—not only in my life but also in the lives of others.*

15

Worship

A gift opens the way for the giver and ushers him
into the presence of the great.

Proverbs 18:16

There's one more discipline that I hope you will add to
your pinpoint praying for yourself. It's the beautiful discipline of worship. When combined with biblical and specific
praying, worship becomes a powerful tool in the hands of an
intercessor. As you will see in this chapter, worship doesn't
just attract God's heart; it changes yours. I have found that
sometimes all the pinpoint praying that I need to do can be
accomplished through passionate worship. If you don't currently have the disciplines of private and corporate worship
built into your life, I believe you will want to after reading
this chapter.

Jailhouse Rock

The prisoners in the dungeon in Philippi couldn't believe what they were hearing. They had heard many sounds bounce off those prison walls—the cries of the tortured, the pleas for mercy, the angry curses, the pathetic and lonely whimpers at night—but this was a new one. It was singing. And it wasn't just singing; it was worship.

Paul and his missionary partner, Silas, had been arrested without cause in Philippi, beaten mercilessly, and then locked in stocks in the jail's dungeon. In spite of the pain of their wounds, and in response to their present circumstances, the two Christ-followers decided that only one course of action was appropriate—praise. They decided to fill their environment with all-out worship of their holy God. So they started singing. They began to bless and praise the name of the Lord Jesus through singing. That's an unusual strategy for dealing with difficulty, but it worked.

Luke tells us what happened: "About midnight Paul and Silas were praying and singing hymns to God, and the other prisoners were listening to them. Suddenly there was such a violent earthquake that the foundations of the prison were shaken. At once all the prison doors flew open, and everybody's chains came loose" (Acts 16:25–26). I can't tell you how much that passage fires me up. It tells me just how potent and powerful praise can be.

Paul and Silas no doubt wanted out of jail. They also wanted justice for the undeserved treatment they had received. As the night had worn on, they certainly could have engaged in some serious pinpoint praying. But they decided to precede their praying with worship, and that's when the power of God fell. The Lord shook the prison, Paul and Silas were immediately freed, and the jailer and his family ended up believing in Christ. That's quite a turnaround. But that's what worship does—it shakes things up, it breaks the chains of bondage, and it pulls people to Jesus.

God's Living Room

In Isaiah 6, the prophet was given a rare glimpse into the inner throne room of heaven. God, in his mercy, pulled back the curtain of heaven and allowed Isaiah to see the environment in which he is most at home. Isaiah's own words tell us the breathtaking scene he witnessed:

> In the year that King Uzziah died, I saw the Lord seated on a throne, high and exalted, and the train of his robe filled the temple. Above him were seraphs, each with six wings: With two wings they covered their faces, with two they covered their feet, and with two they were flying. And they were calling to one another: "Holy, holy, holy is the LORD Almighty; the whole earth is full of his glory."
>
> Isaiah 6:1–3

Isaiah saw God in his most natural state. He saw God in his "living room." He saw God reigning on a throne. He saw God as the center of attention. And he heard the song that was sung to God without end: "Holy, holy, holy."

Now fast-forward about eight hundred years. The aged disciple John is in exile on the island of Patmos. He, like Isaiah, was allowed to see into the throne room of heaven. What did he see? Not much had changed in God's living room in the eight centuries since Isaiah's vision. John tells us what he witnessed:

> At once I was in the Spirit, and there before me was a throne in heaven with someone sitting on it. And the one who sat there had the appearance of jasper and carnelian. . . .

Each of the four living creatures had six wings and was covered with eyes all around, even under his wings. Day and night they never stop saying: "Holy, holy, holy is the Lord God Almighty, who was, and is, and is to come."

Revelation 4:2–3, 8

John saw very much the same room that Isaiah saw. There was a beautiful throne room. There was a throne with God seated on it. And there was unceasing praise to God. The spiritual beings in his presence were even singing the same song: "Holy, holy, holy."

So what do these two visions tell us about God? They tell us that God is most at home in an atmosphere of praise. They tell us that it is appropriate for God always to be the center of attention. And they tell us that there is never a bad or inappropriate time to worship God. He is always higher and more significant than our circumstances.

When you sit down to pray for yourself, if you will begin with a time of heartfelt and passionate praise to God, you'll find that his presence will become very real to you, and you'll have much more clarity and direction as you pray.

Worship Invites the Presence of God

When Paul and Silas started worshiping God in that dungeon, they were actually inviting the very presence of God into the dungeon with them. Let me explain what I mean.

There is a difference between God's omnipresence (God being everywhere at all times) and God's manifest presence (God demonstrating his power and glory in your circumstances). Before Paul and Silas started singing, God by his very nature was already with them. No dungeon walls can lock out God. God is everywhere, including right there with you as you read these words. That's his omnipresence. But when those two radical disciples started worshiping, God's presence with them moved to a more powerful, tangible level.

When you say things such as "God showed up," "God's Spirit was really with us," or "It felt like wall-to-wall God," you're talking about God's manifest presence. When you are pinpoint praying for your words, for faith and courage, and for the gift of irrelevance, you want the glorious, intensely personal presence of God with you. Invite him into your prayers through your praise. His manifest presence will change your environment.

Let me give you an example. In August of 1976, a deadly flash flood raged through the Big Thompson Canyon, just west of Loveland, Colorado. In the hours just after sunset, a twenty-foot wall of water came hurtling down the narrow canyon, taking out bridges, homes, propane tanks, trees, and, tragically, people. One hundred fifty people died that night.

Christian author and speaker Ney Bailey was on a retreat in the Big Thompson Canyon with several of her fellow staffers from Campus Crusade for Christ. When they heard the warning sirens, Ney and her friends immediately rushed out of their riverside cabin to flee to higher ground. Ney and several others ran out the back door, the one facing the canyon's wall. The seven others who went out the front door facing the river never made it. They were immediately swept away by the raging waters.

Ney and her surviving friends scrambled as far up the wet mountainside as they could. They huddled together in the driving rain and waited for rescue. Before them was a horrifying scene. Through the lightning flashes, they could see cars being carried down the river, their headlights shooting randomly into the night and their occupants still trapped inside. They heard the hiss of propane gas leaking into the air as tanks that had been torn from their foundations were carried along as well. Occasionally they would see an entire cabin, or part of one, being washed downstream.

So how do you pray for yourself in that type of setting? How do you even find the courage to pray? For Ney and her companions, their kingdom instincts just kicked in. The group of ladies started singing. They started worshiping. They began declaring that Jesus was Lord, even in that canyon crisis. As they did, God met them on that mountainside. He comforted and encouraged them. And like Paul and Silas's songs of praise two thousand years earlier, their worship spilled out and affected lives all around them. Their songs and prayers drifted along the canyon walls, and somehow other survivors heard them over the torrent of rain and floodwater. Men and women—some clutching boulders, others stranded in trees—actually began to leave their perches of safety and make their way toward the singing voices. As Ney and her friends continued singing, their little group began to increase in number as flood victims, some who actually risked their lives, clambered to be near this unusual safe haven in the midst of their storm.[1]

What canyon crisis are you facing? What pinpoint prayers for deliverance are you lifting up to God? Add praise to your prayers. God will meet you there.

Worship Attracts God's Power

Paul and Silas also showed us another important principle about mingling worship with pinpoint prayers: praise invites God's power. I hope you see the cause and effect of this principle: worship invites God's manifest presence, and God's presence yields his power.

In 2 Chronicles 20, we read about a crisis facing King Jehoshaphat and the nation of Judah. Three nations had joined together to fight against the people of God. Because of their impending invasion, Jehoshaphat wisely called his nation to fasting and prayer. God heard their prayers and gave this great promise to the king: "Do not be afraid or discouraged because of this vast army. For the battle is not yours, but God's. . . . You will not have to fight this battle. Take up your positions; stand firm and see the deliverance the LORD will give you, O Judah and Jerusalem" (2 Chron. 20:15, 17).

Jehoshaphat took God at his word. The next day, he ordered his army to march out and face the invading horde. But he added an unusual command: "Jehoshaphat appointed men to sing to the LORD and to praise him for the splendor of his holiness as they went out at the head of the army, saying: "Give thanks to the LORD, for his love endures forever" (v. 21). How's that for a battle strategy! The king sent the choir out first, armed only with the praises of God. And God honored the king's faith: "As they began to sing and praise, the LORD set ambushes against the men of Ammon and Moab and Mount Seir who were invading Judah, and they were defeated" (v. 22). Jehoshaphat's strategy reminds me of something David wrote in the Psalms: "May the praise of God be in their mouths and a double-edged sword in their hands" (Ps. 149:6).

Sometimes praise and worship are the most important weapons we have in spiritual warfare. God will bless your praise with his manifest presence. He will show up in your circumstances, no matter how difficult they may be. And where God's holy, manifest presence is, his power is never far behind. God responded to the praises of Judah by granting his presence and sending his power. And by doing so, he answered their pinpoint prayers for deliverance.

Learning to Worship

I believe that worship is a learned discipline. Unless you were fortunate enough to grow up in a church culture that taught and modeled both personal and corporate worship, you may have to teach yourself how to passionately bless God. But don't be intimidated—God wants you to learn to be a worshiper. John 4:23–24 tells us that God is seeking worshipers. He wants you to know how to worship him. Stop right now and pray a pinpoint prayer that you will learn to worship. Pray that Psalm 34:1 would be true for you: "I will praise the Lord at all times. I will constantly speak his praises" (NLT). That's a pinpoint prayer that God will answer!

One of the best ways to build worship into your habit of pinpoint praying is by using your Bible. God's Word isn't just a great guide for praying; it's a great prompter for worship. You can easily take many of the psalms and turn them into direct praises to God.

I like to read a psalm aloud to God. Whenever I see a third-person reference to God in the text (for example, "God is good" or "He is good"), I change it to second person ("You are good"). Praise isn't just talking *about* God's holy character; it is talking *to* God about his holy character. So take passages of Scripture and make them as personal and direct as you can. You'll find that you feel closer to God, and you will sense more of his presence as you begin your pinpoint praying by loving and honoring him.

One of the best ready-to-read passages in the Bible for worshiping God is in 1 Chronicles 29. It's already written directly to God. Try reading it out loud. Offer it right now as a prayer of worship and adoration:

> Praise be to you, O Lord,
> God of our father Israel,

from everlasting to everlasting.
Yours, O LORD, is the greatness and the power
     and the glory and the majesty and the splendor,
     for everything in heaven and earth is yours.
     Yours, O LORD, is the kingdom;
     you are exalted as head over all.
Wealth and honor come from you;
     you are the ruler of all things.
     In your hands are strength and power
     to exalt and give strength to all.
Now, our God, we give you thanks,
     and praise your glorious name.

1 Chronicles 29:10–13

I can't read that passage to God and not feel both humbled and more in love with him. After offering some prayers like that to God, your heart will be in a great place to approach him with your pinpoint prayers.

In appendix B, I've provided three Psalms that I have reworded from third person (about God) to second person (to God). They are three of my favorites to pray to God in my own worship times. I think they will encourage you and show you how easy it is to restate many of the Psalms directly to God.

Pray for a Worshipful Heart

There's one more way to learn to become a worshiper, and I've already mentioned it—pray about it. Offer pinpoint prayers to God that you will become a bold and passionate worshiper of his name. Pray that you will be uninhibited when it comes to honoring God and applauding his name. Make Psalm 44:8 a pinpoint prayer for yourself: *Father, teach me to boast in you all day long.*

I started praying about my own worship habits years ago. I grew up in a tradition that didn't encourage a lot of open expression of praise to God. Add to that my own insecurities and inhibitions, and I was one weak worshiper. But eventually I began to get convicted about showing more emotion and passion during my kid's Little League game than when singing or reading of Jesus's love and sacrificial death for me. So I began to ask God to free my heart. I prayed Psalm 122:1 for myself: "I was glad when they said to me, 'Let us go to the house of the LORD'" (NASB). I wanted to be excited about opportunities to worship God.

Slowly God began to answer my prayer. I found that I began to long for and enjoy worshiping. My own private times of worship began to last longer and become more involved. And my pinpoint praying really took off. In fact, it was during those years of learning to worship that God taught me the principles of pinpoint praying that I've shared in each of the *Pray Big* books. It was almost as if through worshiping, I learned to pray.

Now, years later, I'm much more open and bold in my worship. But I still have my struggles. At a recent men's retreat for our church, I was sitting on the front row, caught up in a rapturous moment of praise. For a few brief moments I had forgotten that I was in front of about a hundred guys, that I was their pastor, and that many of them were no doubt watching me. My hands were extended high into the air, my face was tilted toward heaven, and my eyes were closed. I was in a sincere moment of love and interaction with Christ.

And then I heard it: *Wow, look at you!* It wasn't a person's voice; it was more of a thought or one of those rogue voices that somehow gets loose in your head. And it wasn't a compliment. *Wow, look at you!* really meant, *What an idiot! Look at yourself. You're making a complete fool of yourself in front of all these men. How will they respect and follow you if you act like such a religious fanatic? Put your hands down and get a grip!* The demon's message couldn't have been any clearer.

For a brief moment I hesitated. My hands fell to my side. I felt shame and embarrassment. Then I heard another voice: *Wow, look at you!* But this time it wasn't a demon. The voice was the Holy Spirit's. And he added, *You're a worshiper!* It was an incredibly beautiful affirmation. In that moment, God showed me that he was pleased with my heartfelt love and adoration of his name. He showed me that he wants and seeks worshipers. He also showed me that praise paves our way into God's presence and invites his holy power.

Set Your Faith Free

Are you a worshiper? Do you know how to throw yourself headlong into the passionate praise of the Holy One who died to set you free? If not, pray a pinpoint prayer that you will learn to worship. Pray that God will set your heart free to love and adore him. Pray that you'll fully understand the connection between blessing God's name and your own pinpoint prayers for yourself. Pray that Psalm 111:1 would describe you: "Praise the LORD! I will give thanks to the LORD with all my heart, in the company of the upright and in the assembly" (NASB).

Appendix A

100 Pinpoint Prayers for Yourself

Here are one hundred pinpoint prayers you can use to jump-start your prayers for yourself. Pray through them regularly. As you do, you'll not only find your heart changing, but you'll also begin to discover your own personal pinpoint prayers as you read God's Word. Happy praying!

1. *Lord, as I tell others about you, show me how to speak and teach me what to say.* Exodus 4:12
2. *Holy Father, I pray for the discernment to know when to stop crying out to you and when to step out in courage and faith.* Exodus 14:15
3. *Lord God, I love you and declare you as my master. I do not ever want to be free from you. Mark me as yours. Seal me as your holy property. Tether me to your holy house. I am your servant for life.* Exodus 21:5–6
4. *Lord, I will do everything your Word commands. I will obey you.* Exodus 24:7

5. *Lord Jesus, if you are pleased with me, teach me your ways so I may know you and continue to find favor with you.* Exodus 33:13

6. *Holy Father, I pray that I will always revere your name, walk in your ways, and love you and serve you with all my heart and soul.* Deuteronomy 10:12

7. *Lord God, help me not to be hard-hearted toward the poor but to be openhanded and generous toward them.* Deuteronomy 15:7–8

8. *Father, I pray that you will give me great success in everything I do.* 1 Samuel 18:14

9. *Lord God, help me to act more wisely than those who don't follow you. I pray that my name will be highly esteemed for your glory.* 1 Samuel 18:30

10. *O Lord, may my heart's desire be glorifying you. Please keep my heart loyal to you.* 1 Chronicles 29:18

11. *Lord, let my delight be in your law, and help me to meditate on it day and night.* Psalm 1:2

12. *Holy God, I pray that my walk will always be blameless, that I will do what is righteous, and that I will speak the truth from my heart.* Psalm 15:2

13. *Lord Jesus, please make my steps secure like the steps of a deer, and enable me to stand securely in the high places. Train me to engage in spiritual warfare, and make me strong for battle.* Psalm 18:33–34

14. *Father, please keep me from willful sins; do not let them rule over me. Then I will be blameless, innocent of great transgression.* Psalm 19:13

15. *Lord God, please give me clean hands and a pure heart. Help me not to lift up my soul to an idol or swear by what is false.* Psalm 24:4

16. *Holy Father, please instruct me and teach me in the way I should go; please counsel me and watch over me.* Psalm 32:8

17. *Mighty God, please keep my tongue from evil and my lips from speaking lies.* Psalm 34:13

18. *Holy Lord, please place your law in my heart and keep my feet from stumbling.* Psalm 37:31

19. *Hear my prayer, O Lord, and listen to my cry for help; do not be deaf to my weeping.* Psalm 39:12

20. *O Lord, have mercy on me and heal me, for I have sinned against you.* Psalm 41:4

21. *Holy God, let my mouth speak words of wisdom; let the reflections of my heart give others understanding.* Psalm 49:3

22. *Lord, teach me to willingly sacrifice to you. Help me to joyfully praise your name, for you are good.* Psalm 54:6

23. *O Father, you are my God; help me to earnestly seek you. Let my soul thirst for you and you alone.* Psalm 63:1

24. *Father, I will be faithful to you. I will keep the promises I have made to you.* Psalm 66:13

25. *Holy Lord, I pray that I would never do anything that would bring embarrassment to your name or shame to those who follow you.* Psalm 69:6

26. *Mighty God, let zeal for your house consume me. Make me zealous for your name and your purpose. Make me a passionate worshiper.* Psalm 69:9

27. *O Lord, teach me your way, and I will walk in your truth. Give me an undivided heart so I will fear your name.* Psalm 86:11

28. *Holy Lord, help me to lead a blameless life. Enable me to walk in my house with a blameless heart. I*

will set no vile or sinful thing before my eyes. Psalm 101:2–3

29. *Lord God, give me a grateful heart. Give me boldness and courage to boast about you to others.* Psalm 111:1

30. *Holy Father, I want to love your law. Help me to meditate on it all day long.* Psalm 119:97

31. *Lord God, thank you for hearing me when I call on you. As I do, please make me bold and courageous.* Psalm 138:3

32. *Lord Jesus, do not let my heart be drawn to what is evil or take part in wicked deeds with men who are evildoers. Do not let me eat of their delicacies.* Psalm 141:4

33. *Lord Jesus, please make my ears attentive to wisdom, and help me apply my heart to understanding.* Proverbs 2:2

34. *Father, let my teaching be wise and a fountain of life. Let my words turn others from the snares of death.* Proverbs 13:14

35. *Lord Jesus, help me to live an upright life, and let my prayers be pleasing to you.* Proverbs 15:8

36. *Holy God, help me be open to a loving rebuke so that I will gain knowledge.* Proverbs 19:25

37. *Father, help me to guard my mouth and my tongue so that I will keep myself from calamity.* Proverbs 21:23

38. *Holy Lord, as you place your calling on my life, may my answer be, "Here I am, send me!"* Isaiah 6:8

39. *Lord God, I pray that your Spirit will rest on me—the Spirit of wisdom and understanding, the Spirit of counsel and power, the Spirit of knowledge and the fear of the Lord. O God, help me to delight in the fear of the Lord.* Isaiah 11:2–3

40. *Father, make me a person of prayer. Help me day and night to keep watch over my family, my church, my city, and my nation through prayer.* Isaiah 21:8

41. *Lord Jesus, please keep me in perfect peace as my mind is steadfast and I trust in you.* Isaiah 26:3

42. *Holy God, please make your name and renown the desire of my heart.* Isaiah 26:8

43. *Lord God, you are my God. Instruct me and teach me the right way.* Isaiah 28:26

44. *Holy Father, guide my steps. Whether I turn to the right or the left, let me hear your voice saying, "This is the way; walk in it."* Isaiah 30:21

45. *Lord Jesus, I seek your forgiveness. For your name's sake, blot out my transgressions and remember my sins no more.* Isaiah 43:25

46. *Holy Lord, please give me an instructed tongue. Teach me to offer words that sustain the weary.* Isaiah 50:4

47. *Lord, I am your servant. Help me to act wisely in all that I do.* Isaiah 52:13

48. *Holy God, make me hungry to worship at your holy mountain, and make me joyful in your house of prayer.* Isaiah 56:7

49. *Lord Jesus, let your mighty Spirit rest on me. Anoint me to preach good news to the poor, to bind up the broken-hearted, to proclaim freedom to captives and release from darkness to prisoners, to proclaim the year of the Lord's favor and the day of vengeance of our God, and to comfort all who mourn.* Isaiah 61:1–2

50. *Holy God, make me humble and contrite in spirit, and help me to tremble at your Word.* Isaiah 66:2

51. *Holy Father, help me to overcome temptation by clinging to the power of your Word.* Matthew 4:1–4

52. *Lord Jesus, please give me the gift of brokenness. Make me poor in spirit so that I will be completely dependent on you and know your kingdom in my life.* Matthew 5:3

53. *Lord Jesus, give me the courage to follow you and to be a fisher of men.* Mark 1:17

54. *Lord God, I pray that when I hear your word and command for my life, I will immediately respond by saying, "So be it! I am the Lord's servant."* Luke 1:38

55. *Holy Father, I know that to whom much has been given, much will be required. You have blessed me with so much! Help me to be a good steward of all that you've given me.* Luke 12:48

56. *Lord Jesus, I pray that you will increase in me and that I will decrease.* John 3:30

57. *Lord Jesus, teach me to follow the example you set for me. As you washed the feet of your disciples, so help me to wash others' feet.* John 13:13–15

58. *Lord God, I pray that you will fill me with your Spirit and enable me to speak your Word boldly.* Acts 4:31

59. *Holy Father, please make me like Stephen—full of faith and of the Holy Spirit.* Acts 6:5

60. *Holy God, help me to see myself as dead to sin but alive to you.* Romans 6:11

61. *Lord Jesus, help me to gladly bear with the failings of the weak and live not to please myself.* Romans 15:1

62. *Father, help me never to eat, drink, say, or do anything that would cause any brother or sister of mine to stumble.* 1 Corinthians 8:13

63. *Father, please show me what spiritual gifts you have given me so that I can use them for the common good of your church.* 1 Corinthians 12:7

64. *Lord God, help me not to see people from a worldly point of view, but teach me to see them through the eyes of Christ.* 2 Corinthians 5:16

65. *Lord Jesus, as you help me to excel in everything—in faith, speech, knowledge, complete earnestness, and love for your church—help me also to excel in the grace of giving.* 2 Corinthians 8:7

66. *Lord God, teach me that I have been crucified with Christ and that I no longer live, but Christ lives in me. Remind me that the life I live in the body, I live by faith in the Son of God, who loved me and gave himself for me.* Galatians 2:20

67. *Lord Jesus, may the fruit of your Spirit—love, joy, peace, patience, kindness, goodness, faithfulness, gentleness, and self-control—be clearly evident in me.* Galatians 5:22–23

68. *Lord Jesus, please continue to give me a spirit of wisdom and revelation so that I can know you better.* Ephesians 1:17

69. *Holy Father, help me to live a life worthy of the calling I have received from you.* Ephesians 4:1

70. *Lord Jesus, I pray that you who began this good work in me will continue it until I see you in heaven.* Philippians 1:6

71. *Father, I pray that you would help my mind to dwell on whatever is true, noble, right, pure, lovely, admirable, excellent, and praiseworthy.* Philippians 4:8

72. *Lord Jesus, help me to rid myself of all anger, rage, malice, slander, and filthy language.* Colossians 3:8

73. *Father, help me to be devoted to prayer, being watchful and thankful.* Colossians 4:2

74. *Father, I pray that my work will be produced by faith, my labor prompted by love, and my endurance inspired by my hope in the Lord Jesus Christ.* 1 Thessalonians 1:3

75. *Lord Jesus, I pray that I would never quench your Spirit's work in my life.* 1 Thessalonians 5:19

76. *Father, I pray that my faith will grow more and more and that my love for others will always be increasing.* 2 Thessalonians 1:3

77. *Lord Jesus, help me never to tire of doing what is right.* 2 Thessalonians 3:13

78. *Holy Father, please give me your strength, find me faithful, and appoint me to your service.* 1 Timothy 1:12

79. *Lord Jesus, thank you for providing for my needs. Please help me to be content with what I have.* 1 Timothy 6:8

80. *Lord Jesus, help me to present myself to God as one approved—a workman who doesn't need to be ashamed and who correctly handles the word of truth.* 2 Timothy 2:15

81. *Holy Father, teach me to flee from all evil desires and pursue righteousness, faith, love, and peace, along with all the rest of those who call on you out of a pure heart.* 2 Timothy 2:22

82. *Lord God, help me to live a life that is above reproach for your glory.* Titus 1:6–7

83. *Father, help me to set a good example for other Christ-followers in everything by doing what is good.* Titus 2:7

84. *Lord Jesus, I pray that my teaching will show integrity, seriousness, and soundness of speech that cannot be condemned, so that those who oppose your kingdom may be*

ashamed because they have nothing bad to say about me. Titus 2:7–8

85. *Lord God, I pray that I may be active in sharing my faith so that I will have a full understanding of every good thing I have in Christ.* Philemon 1:6

86. *Lord Jesus, help me always to fix my thoughts on you.* Hebrews 3:1

87. *Holy Father, by your grace, help me to leave the basics of discipleship and press on to maturity.* Hebrews 6:1

88. *Holy God, give me the courage to be mistreated along with your people rather than enjoy the pleasures of sin for a season.* Hebrews 11:25

89. *Father, help me to regard disgrace for the sake of Christ as of greater value than the treasures of this earth, as I look ahead to my heavenly reward.* Hebrews 11:26

90. *Lord God, since I have received a kingdom that cannot be shaken, help me to be thankful and worship you acceptably with reverence and awe.* Hebrews 12:28

91. *Lord Jesus, I pray for wisdom daily so that I will bring glory to your name.* James 1:5

92. *Father, give me courage to tell others about you so that sinners will turn from the error of their ways, be saved from death, and be forgiven for a multitude of sins.* James 5:20

93. *Lord Jesus, because you are holy, please make me holy.* 1 Peter 1:15

94. *Holy Father, help me to live as a holy priest, offering spiritual sacrifices acceptable to you through Jesus Christ.* 1 Peter 2:5

95. *Lord Jesus, make me a royal priest, that I may declare the praises of him who called me out of darkness into his wonderful light.* 1 Peter 2:9

96. *Mighty God, help me to rely on your great and precious promises so that through them I may participate in the divine nature and escape the corruption in the world caused by evil desires.* 2 Peter 1:4

97. *Lord Jesus, help me to live as you lived, to love as you loved, and to walk as you walked.* 1 John 2:6

98. *Holy Father, I pray that I will love not with words or tongue but with actions and in truth.* 1 John 3:18

99. *Lord God, teach me to build myself up in our most holy faith and to pray in your Holy Spirit. Help me always to keep myself in your love.* Jude 1:20–21

100. *Lord Jesus, help me to be merciful to those who doubt, to snatch others from the fire and save them, to show mercy to others, and to hate even the clothing stained by corrupted flesh.* Jude 1:22–23

Appendix B

Psalms of Praise

Here are three ready-to-read psalms of praise. Read them out loud to God. Then start writing your own!

Psalm 23—Lord, you are my shepherd; I shall not be in want. You make me lie down in green pastures, you lead me beside quiet waters, and you restore my soul. You guide me in paths of righteousness for your name's sake. Even though I walk through the valley of the shadow of death, I will fear no evil, for you are with me; your rod and your staff, they comfort me. You prepare a table before me in the presence of my enemies. You anoint my head with oil; my cup overflows. Surely goodness and love will follow me all the days of my life, and I will dwell in your house forever, O Lord.

Psalm 111—I will praise you, Lord, with all my heart, in the council of the upright and in the assembly. Great are your works, O Lord; they are pondered by all who delight in them. Glorious and majestic are your deeds, and your righteousness endures forever. You have caused your wonders to be remembered. Lord, you are gracious and compassionate. You provide food for those who fear you; you remember your covenant forever. You have shown your people the power of your works, giving them the lands of other nations.

The works of your hands are faithful and just; all your precepts are trustworthy. They are steadfast forever and ever, done in faithfulness and uprightness. You provided redemption for your people; you ordained your covenant forever. Holy and awesome is your name. To fear you, Lord, is the beginning of wisdom; all who follow your precepts have good understanding. To you belongs eternal praise.

Psalm 145—I will exalt you, my God the King; I will praise your name forever and ever. Every day I will praise you and extol your name forever and ever. Great are you, Lord, and most worthy of praise; your greatness no one can fathom. One generation will commend your works to another; they will tell of your mighty acts. They will speak of the glorious splendor of your majesty, and I will meditate on your wonderful works. They will tell of the power of your awesome works, and I will proclaim your great deeds. They will celebrate your abundant goodness and joyfully sing of your righteousness.

Lord, you are gracious and compassionate, slow to anger and rich in love. You are good to all; you have compassion on all you have made. All you have made will praise you, O Lord; your saints will extol you. They will tell of the glory of your kingdom and speak of your might, so that all men may know of your mighty acts and the glorious splendor of your kingdom. Your kingdom is an everlasting kingdom, and your dominion endures through all generations.

Lord, you are faithful to all your promises and loving toward all you have made. You uphold all those who fall and lift up all who are bowed down. The eyes of all look to you, and you give them their food at the proper time. You open your hand and satisfy the desires of every living thing.

Lord, you are righteous in all your ways and loving toward all you have made. You are near to all who call on you in truth. You fulfill the desires of those who fear you; you hear their cries and save them. Lord, you watch over all who love you, but you will destroy all the wicked. My mouth will speak praise to you, O Lord. Let every creature praise your holy name forever and ever.

Reflection Questions

Chapter 1: Tired of Just Hanging Around?

1. Describe your current habits of praying for yourself. Do you pray frequently or infrequently? What do you pray for? Do you feel that it's selfish to pray for yourself?

2. This chapter listed three reasons that we should pray for ourselves. Which of those reasons for personal prayer make the most sense for your life right now? Why?

3. How will you respond to the invitation to cut the rope that ties you to spiritual complacency and begin the adventure of praying for yourself?

4. After reading this chapter, how will you pray differently for yourself?

Chapter 2: Set Your Prayers on Fire

1. Before reading this chapter, had you ever heard of the concept of pinpoint praying or of praying the Scriptures? If so, what are some of the verses you pray most often to God?

2. What are two key ingredients in pinpoint prayers?

3. Why do you think prayers that contain those ingredients are so powerful?

4. The Lord's Prayer serves as a basis for pinpoint prayers in five areas of our lives: perspective, priorities, provision, pardon, and protection. Which one do you relate to the most? Which do you most need to pray for your life?

5. After reading this chapter, how will you pray differently for yourself?

Chapter 3: Finding Buried Treasure

1. What is your favorite Bible verse? In the space below, try writing your favorite verse as a prayer to God.

2. Take a look at the following verses. In the space provided, express each of them as a pinpoint prayer.
   • Psalm 23:1: "The LORD is my shepherd, I shall not be in want."

   • Jeremiah 24:7: "I will give them a heart to know me, that I am the LORD. They will be my people, and I will be their God, for they will return to me with all their heart."

- Colossians 3:1–2: "Since, then, you have been raised with Christ, set your hearts on things above, where Christ is seated at the right hand of God. Set your minds on things above, not on earthly things."

3. This chapter listed four questions to ask to determine if a verse might become one of your pinpoint prayers. Which question seems to be the most important for you to ask, and why?

4. What pinpoint promises does God want you to start praying for your life?

5. After reading this chapter, how will you pray differently for yourself?

Chapter 4: Arm in Arm with Jesus

1. List four or five synonyms for *proximity*.

2. How well do those words describe your relationship with Jesus? Are you close to him—so close that you can hear his heartbeat? Or are you like Peter was at times, following at a distance?

3. How can you tell if you are close to Jesus or not?

4. John 15 talks about the importance of abiding in Christ. Would you describe yourself as an abiding Christian? If not, what would it take for you to become one?

5. After reading this chapter, how will you pray differently for yourself?

Chapter 5: No Delay

1. Rate your obedience response time (ORT) on a scale of 1 to 5, with 1 being stalled or slow obedience, and 5 being immediate obedience.

2. Can you recall a time when you delayed your obedience to God and it cost you or others something? What happened?

3. Can you recall a time when you obeyed God and he honored it? What happened?

4. Why is obedience scary? What keeps so many of us from practicing immediate obedience to God?

5. After reading this chapter, how will you pray differently for yourself?

Chapter 6: Did I Just Say That?

1. Think of a time when you said something you immediately regretted. What did you say, and what happened?

2. The tongue seems like such a small thing, but both Testaments of the Bible talk about how damaging it can be. What does that tell you about how important it is to God that we control our tongues?

3. Read Ephesians 4:29 and think about how your words can be used to build up others. Be as specific as you can.

4. After reading this chapter, how will you pray differently for yourself?

Chapter 7: More Blessed

1. Would you describe yourself as a generous person? Why or why not? Is giving money to your church or other ministries a priority? Why or why not?

2. What reasons do people give today for not giving to churches? List as many as you can, and be as specific as you can.

3. This chapter mentioned several benefits of and reasons for giving. Which do you think is most important or compelling? Why?

4. What do you think would happen in your life if you started praying for a generous spirit? How might your life be different?

5. After reading this chapter, how will you pray differently for yourself?

Chapter 8: In Jesus's Name

1. Think about the description of oppression at the beginning of the chapter. After reading it, do you think you've ever been oppressed? When? What happened?

2. When you were being oppressed, how did you feel? At what point did you realize you were being oppressed? How did you realize it?

3. What is the basis of a believer's authority over Satan? What right or power do we have to command Satan to leave us alone?

4. Which of the three pinpoint prayers in this chapter was most meaningful to you, and why?

5. After reading this chapter, how will you pray differently for yourself?

Chapter 9: How to Move a Mountain

1. Think about a time when your faith has really been tested. What happened?

2. What do you think about the statement in this chapter that says, "If you're a Christian, you already have more than a mustard seed's worth of faith"? How does it make you feel?

3. If you had more faith, what would you be doing today that you're currently not doing?

4. After reading this chapter, how will you pray differently for yourself?

Chapter 10: Get Out of the Boat

1. In your own words, define *faith* and *courage*. How are those words related? What are the differences between them?

2. Rate your level of courage on a scale of 1 to 5, with 1 being little courage and 5 being radical, never-hesitate-in-following-God courage.

3. Can you name a time when God led you to step out in faith? Did you have the courage to obey him? What happened?

4. What do you think would happen if you prayed for more courage?

5. After reading this chapter, how will you pray differently for yourself?

Chapter 11: I Must Become Less

1. Why does praying for the gift of irrelevance seem so counterintuitive? What's scary about seeking to be obscure?

2. John 3:30 says, "He must increase; but I must decrease" (NASB). Restate that verse in your own words.

3. Why is it a good and biblical thing for you to pray for irrelevance?

4. How might you be different if you started praying to decrease so Jesus could increase? What attitudes, conflicts, and struggles might change if you let go of trying to be important? What temptations might you avoid?

5. After reading this chapter, how will you pray differently for yourself?

Chapter 12: Learning the Bible

1. On how many days were you able to spend time reading the Bible in the last week? What could you change in your routine to protect or increase your Bible-reading time?

2. Think of a Bible verse that you know by heart. How did you learn it? When did you learn it?

3. Say the following verse several times out loud: "Therefore, there is now no condemnation for those who are in Christ Jesus" (Rom. 8:1). Emphasize a different word every time you say the verse. If you're in a group, have each group member emphasize a different word. How does repeating the verse and emphasizing each word help you understand its meaning?

4. How would knowing the Bible better enhance your pinpoint praying?

5. After reading this chapter, how will you pray differently for yourself?

Chapter 13: Spiritual Breathing

1. In your own words, describe the discipline known as spiritual breathing.

2. Which verse would you say best describes the current status of your relationship with God: Isaiah 59:2 ("But your iniquities have separated you from your God; your sins have hidden his face from you, so that he will not hear"), or 1 John 1:9 ("If we confess our sins, he is faithful and just and will forgive us our sins and purify us from all unrighteousness"). Why?

3. Think of a recent time when you got into an argument, got angry at someone else, or made a poor decision that basically ruined the rest of your day. What happened? Now, think about the principles involved in spiritual breathing. How might that situation have ended differently if you had confessed it immediately and sought the filling of God's Spirit? Be as specific as you can.

4. After reading this chapter, how will you pray differently for yourself?

Chapter 14: Fasting

1. Have you ever fasted? If so, why? What type of experience did you have?

2. Which of the benefits of fasting is most attractive to you? Why?

3. What area in your life—a relationship, a sin, an upcoming decision, a need—might God want you to fast

about? What do you think would happen if you chose to fast about it?

4. After reading this chapter, how will you pray differently for yourself?

Chapter 15: Worship

1. In your own words, define *worship*.

2. Which story about worship in this chapter moves you the most, and why? What do you learn about worship from these examples?

3. Describe a profound or meaningful experience you had in worship. How did it affect you? If you've never had a profound worship moment, why do you think you haven't? What would have to change for you to become more engaged in worship?

4. How do you think worship will help your pinpoint praying for yourself?

5. After reading this chapter, how will you pray differently for yourself?

Notes

Chapter 2: Set Your Prayers on Fire

1. For the full account of this event, see Matthew 21:12–13 and John 2:13–17.

2. *Pray Big* (Grand Rapids: Revell, 2007), *Pray Big for Your Marriage* (Grand Rapids: Revell, 2008), *Pray Big for Your Child* (Grand Rapids: Revell, 2009).

3. Rick Bragg, "Prisoner's Pittance Is Meant as Reminder of a Great Loss," *New York Times*, December 26, 1996.

Chapter 3: Finding Buried Treasure

1. Gary Detman, "Bible Survives Devastating Fire," Firstcoastnews.com, 2008, http://www.firstcoastnews.com/news/florida/news-article.aspx?storyid=104722.

2. In appendix A, I have provided one hundred pinpoint prayers. You'll find them to be timeless and relevant. Pray them for yourself as long as they're helpful, or at least until you've developed an ability to discover your own pinpoint prayers.

Chapter 4: Arm in Arm with Jesus

1. A great source of pinpoint prayers for loving and obeying God's Word is Psalm 119.

Chapter 7: More Blessed

1. The Barna Update, "New Study Shows Trends in Tithing and Donating," The Barna Group, April 14, 2008, http://www.barna.org/FlexPage.aspx?Page=BarnaUpdate&BarnaUpdateID=296.

2. Joel Belz, "Our 2 Cents' Worth," *World Magazine*, October 27, 2007, 3.

3. See Huck Gutman, "Economic Inequality in US," July 1, 2002, http://www.commondreams.org/views02/0701-05.htm; and BBC News, "Why Does the US

Need Our Money?" September 6, 2005, http://news.bbc.co.uk/2/hi/uk_news/magazine/4215336.stm.

4. Randolph Schmid, "Better to Give than Receive? Even Science Can't Argue with That," *Austin American-Statesman*, March 21, 2008.

Chapter 10: Get Out of the Boat

1. Garrison Keillor, "My Five Most Important Books," *Newsweek*, December 24, 2007, 17.

Chapter 11: I Must Become Less

1. Oswald Chambers, *My Utmost for His Highest*, February 5 entry, http://www.myutmost.org/02/0205.html.

Chapter 14: Fasting

1. Bill Bright, *Seven Basic Steps to Successful Fasting and Prayer* (Orlando, FL: Bright Media Foundation and Campus Crusade for Christ, 2007). This little book is also available to read on the Internet. Go to www.billbright.com/7steps, or you can order it from www.campuscrusade.com.

2. Art Wallis, *God's Chosen Fast* (Fort Washington, PA: Christian Literature Crusade, 1980).

Chapter 15: Worship

1. For the full amazing account of this story, see Ney Bailey, *Faith Is Not a Feeling* (Colorado Springs, CO: WaterBrook Press, 2002).

Will Davis Jr. is the founding and senior pastor of Austin Christian Fellowship in Austin, Texas. Will and his wife, Susie, have three children.

A Note from the Editors

This book was specially selected by the editors of the Books and Inspirational Media Division of Guideposts, a nonprofit organization that touches millions of lives every day through products and services that inspire, encourage and uplift. Our magazines, books and outreach programs help people connect their faith-filled values to daily life.

Your purchase of this book makes a difference. When you buy Guideposts products, you're helping fund our many outreach programs to military personnel, prisons, hospitals, nursing homes and educational institutions.

To learn more about our outreach ministry, visit GuidepostsFoundation.org. To find out about our other publications such as *Daily Guideposts*, and to enjoy free online resources such as inspirational newsletters, blogs and videos, visit Guideposts.org. You can also write to us at Guideposts, PO Box 5815, Harlan, Iowa 51593.